FOCAL CINEBOOKS

HOW TO FILM
by G. Wain

HOW TO SCRIPT
by Oswell Blakeston

HOW TO DIRECT
by Tony Rose

HOW TO PROJECT
by Norman Jenkins

HOW TO TITLE
by L. F. Minter

HOW TO PROCESS
by Leslie Wheeler

HOW TO USE COLOUR
by C. L. Thomson

HOW TO CARTOON
by J. Halas & B. Privett

HOW TO EDIT
by H. Baddeley

HOW TO ACT
by Tony Rose & Martin Benson

HOW TO USE 9.5 mm.
by D. M. Neale

HOW TO MAKE HOLIDAY FILMS
by H. Baddeley

HOW TO MAKE 8 mm. FILMS
by N. Bau

HOW TO WRITE FILM STORIES
by R. Harrison

HOW TO ADD SOUND
by D. M. Neale

HOW TO PRODUCE EFFECTS
by Julien Caunter

HOW TO DO TRICKS
by Julien Caunter

HOW TO FILM CHILDREN
by M. Natkin

HOW TO WRITE COMMENTARIES
by M. Kirsch

HOW TO CHOOSE MUSIC
by F. Rawlings

HOW TO ANIMATE CUT-OUTS
by C. H. Barton

Each 7/6 net

Translated and adapted from the French by
R. Howard Cricks, F.B.K.S., F.R.P.S.
with the authorization of
*Publications Photographiques et Cinématographiques
Paul Montel, Paris.*

First published in 1954

Second edition 1955

Third edition 1956

Fourth edition 1957

Printed 1957 in Great Britain by Billing and Sons, Ltd., Guildford and
London, for The Focal Press Ltd., 31, Fitzroy Square, London, W.1.

N. Bau

How to Make

8 mm. FILMS

as an amateur

Fourth Edition

FOCAL PRESS
London and New York

Contents

3

5

Eight mm. Cine Film

MANY of us take snapshots to record happy occasions, memories of places visited, or the faces of people we know. All these really come to life much more in a moving film projected on the screen.

We all too often tend to associate moving pictures with luxury cinemas and Hollywood mammoth productions. Yet we have the animated equivalent of casual snapshots well within our reach—in 8 mm. narrow-gauge film. Unlike the larger, and thus more expensive, motion-picture film sizes, it is the true medium of informal and intimate film-making for everybody.

The film we are going to employ is 8 mm., or about $\frac{5}{16}$ inch in width. It carries a sequence of cine pictures or frames which, projected on a screen in rapid succession, produce a living picture of the scene that was in front of our camera.

The frames are the smallest photographic images used, and measure 0.19×0.14 inch (4.8×3.5 mm.). The area projected is in fact slightly smaller still, owing to the gate aperture of the projector, and measures 0.17×0.13 inch (4.37×3.28 mm.). Certainly the difference is very slight, but when the image is enlarged several hundred times in area upon the screen every thousandth of an inch counts!

Advantages of 8 mm.

The 8 mm. film has many practical advantages.

1. It is inexpensive. A single $2\frac{1}{4} \times 3\frac{1}{4}$ inch still photograph costs about the same as an animated scene lasting 10 seconds. And it is a still photograph, compared with living pictures viewed on a screen a yard wide! There is no

7

question that the moving picture is far more interesting to watch than a single photograph on paper.

We can push the comparison further, by looking at the cost of a quarter-plate photograph in colour and a colour film lasting 10 seconds in the projector: the moving film is actually cheaper than the still picture in colour.

2. 8 mm. film is internationally obtainable. In every country throughout the world, it is possible to buy 8 mm. film, and to have it processed without additional cost. For example, if you buy an 8 mm. film from an English chemist, you can have it developed in any part of the world by the manufacturer's laboratory.

The film is processed (without charge) by a technique standardised by the manufacturers or by one of their laboratories.

3. It is simple to load. You buy the film on a spool or charger with a leader at each end of the length to be exposed. You slip the film into the camera in daylight, just as you would load a roll-film camera.

4. You have different types of emulsions. You can use highly sensitive film for shooting in very bad light or in winter, or slower films when the light is good.

In colour, there is one emulsion for daylight and another for artificial lighting by over-run lamps.

There is one point of difference between 8 mm. film and still film. Your still film when it comes back from processing is a negative; it is the prints made from these negatives that are positives. But with 8 mm. there is no negative: the film you expose in your camera is processed directly to a positive, and you run in your projector the actual film which you exposed in your camera, so saving the cost of a second film.

You can, however, still have duplicates made of your 8 mm. film.

Although the film you project measures exactly 8 mm. in width, for taking you can use two different types of raw stock. Each type is made to suit a distinct type of camera.

8

Double-eight Film

The majority of cameras use double-eight film for taking. This film is 16 mm. (roughly $\frac{5}{8}$ inch) in width, with perforations on both sides. The actual usable length of the normal packing is 25 feet, but at the beginning and end are lengths of leader film, intended for the loading and reloading of the camera in daylight. These leaders are of course fogged, and are not counted in development, as they are cut off at the processing laboratory.

Some types of camera will carry either 25 feet spools or 50 and 100 feet cassettes. Like the shorter reels, these also carry leaders at either end.

The extra length is useful during a long voyage, or for filming surgical operations and in scientific research.

How Double-eight Film is Exposed

If you look at a piece of double-eight film, you will see that it has a large number of perforations along each edge. Between each pair of perforations we are going to expose a picture about $\frac{3}{16}$ inch in width and $\frac{1}{8}$ inch in height.

Double-eight film (here approx. 2¼ times natural size) runs twice through the camera and thus carries two sets of images. After development the strip is slit down the middle to give two single-eight lengths.

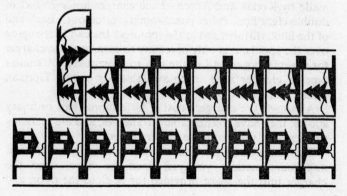

First, half the width of the film is exposed—that is to say, a width of about $\frac{3}{16}$ inch. The second half remains unexposed until later. After the first half of the film has been exposed for its whole length, the spools are changed round to expose the second half of the film.

To do this, first remove from the camera the take-up spool which carries the half-exposed film, pull off the now empty feed spool, and place it on the take-up spindle. Then put the spool of half-exposed film on the feed spindle, and carry on shooting.

After exposure, the film is sent to the maker or his laboratories for processing. There it is slit in two along its length, and the two halves are joined together. From a 25 feet spool of double-eight film you get a 50 feet length of film for projection.

If you project this film at a speed of 16 frames per second, it will run for 4 minutes. On that basis, the 50 feet double-eight film gives 100 feet after processing, which will run for 8 minutes. The 100 feet double-eight reel will give 16 minutes of projecting at normal speed.

Double-eight Chargers

Several American cameras use a special type of charger made by Kodak and Ansco. Each charger holds 25 feet of double-eight film, either panchromatic or colour. Each end of the film is firmly fixed to the spindles. Instead of changing over the spools, it is only necessary to turn over the charger for the unexposed half of the film to be exposed. A similar type of charger used to be available for certain German 8 mm. cameras.

Although the chargers cost a little more than ordinary spools, they have considerable advantages, and are certainly preferred by users of these camera types.

The insertion of the film into the camera is made easier and more certain—you just open the door, drop the charger into the space provided for it, close the door, and the camera is ready to run. At the end of the first run, open the camera, reverse the charger, and continue taking.

Loading is quicker—there is no waste of time in running through the lead, no risk of fogging of the edges of the first half of the film, no risk of jamming due to incorrect loading, or to the film coming off the take-up spindle.

The beginning and end of the film are clearly marked; you are always certain that the scenes exposed are not fogged or cut.

Single-eight Film

As its name indicates, single-eight film differs from double-eight in that the camera film measures only 8 mm. in width, and has only a single row of perforations.

Single-eight film is always supplied in special 30 feet chargers, which remain the property of the film-maker.

Single-eight film, like double-eight, is always sold inclusive of processing charges, processing being carried out by the maker of the film.

The single-eight charger has roughly the same advantages as the American magazines in regard to ease of loading, and freedom from accidents during taking. The same types of emulsions are available in single-eight, although there are more different makes.

FILM GAUGES COMPARED

Data	8 mm.	9.5 mm. silent	16 mm.	
Image size on film	0.19×0.14	0.35×0.26	0.41×0.29	in.
	4.8 ×3.5	8.8 ×6.5	10.4 ×7.5	mm.
Centre distance between frames	0.16	0.29	0.30	in.
	3.8	7.5	7.6	mm.
Picture area	0.026	0.089	0.12	sq. in.
	16.9	57	78	sq. mm.
Frames per foot ...	80	40	40	
Feet screened per minute at 16 f.p.s.	12	24	24	

Optical Camera Features

To obtain best results from any camera you must know just how it works. The main features of a cine camera fall under three distinct headings:

1. The optical system, including the lens and viewfinder;
2. The mechanical parts, comprising the motor and its controls; and
3. The film feeding system and its components.

The Lens

The job of the lens or objective is to form a photographic image on the film. Because of the small size of this image, lenses for cine cameras must have very definite properties, and must be of the highest quality.

If you examine the normal lens supplied with the camera, you will see that it carries the following markings: 12.5 mm. (sometimes 12 mm., sometimes $\frac{1}{2}$ inch) focal length, or abbreviated $f = 12.5$ mm. The focal length governs the angle of view that your camera lens covers, and determines the scale of the image produced.

In still photography the focal length of a normal camera lens is equal to, or slightly greater than, the diagonal of the frame. This diagonal for an 8 mm. film is about 6.5 mm. (roughly $\frac{1}{4}$ inch). But in the cine camera the focal length of the normal lens is twice this theoretical value, or about 12.5 mm. or $\frac{1}{2}$ inch. This is the case with all gauges of film —8 mm., 9.5 mm., 16 mm., and equally in the professional 35 mm. gauge.

As a result, the angle of view of your cine camera is only half that of a still camera. This is why, when a still photographer uses a cine camera for the first time, he is astonished at the small field covered, and is inclined to work at too great a distance in order to be able to see the subject in his viewfinder.

The Speed of a Lens

· The brightest image that can be formed by a lens depends upon the largest opening or aperture of the iris, and is expressed in what is known as the *f* value. The lower the *f* value, the larger the aperture. For example, the widest aperture lens at present obtainable works at *f* 1.4 (marked on Continental lenses as 1 : 1.4). Most good lenses work at *f* 1.9; this is the type of lens found in the majority of cameras. Simpler and less expensive lenses, whether in a fixed mount or interchangeably mounted, work at *f* 2.8.

Besides the marking showing the largest aperture of the lens, the iris ring carries markings which represent the smaller iris openings. These apertures may follow one of two scales:

APERTURE SCALES

International scale	1.4	2	2.8	4	5.6	8	11	16
Continental scale ...	1.6	2.2	3.2	4.5	6.3	9	12.5	18

Often the largest aperture (e.g., *f* 1.9) does not fit into either system.

The numbers 16 and 18 indicate the smallest openings of the iris, and the lowest numbers the full aperture. Between these limits are markings so arranged that in stopping down from say *f* 8 to *f* 11 or from *f* 9 to *f* 12.5 the amount of light entering the camera is halved. Conversely, in opening up from *f* 8 to *f* 5.6 (or *f* 9 to *f* 6.3) the amount of light is doubled.

B—C

Fixed-focus Lenses

In theory, we have to adjust the lens, or focus it according to the distance of the subject we are filming, in order to achieve maximum sharpness. But in practice, with the medium aperture lens of a simple camera the depth of field, or the zone of sharpness (p. 15), is very great. Such cameras therefore often have fixed-focus lenses. In good conditions of lighting, when the light is bright enough to permit the lens being stopped down, the fixed-focus lens gives a zone of sharpness which theoretically extends from infinity to the following distances from the camera:

ZONES OF SHARPNESS WITH FIXED-FOCUS LENSES

Aperture ... ... f	2.8	4	5.6	8	11	16
Nearest sharp point ft.	$6\frac{1}{2}$	5	4	3	$2\frac{1}{2}$	2
m.	2	1.5	1.2	0.9	0.75	0.6

These distances apply only to lenses of a focal length of 12–13 mm. or $\frac{1}{2}$ inch.

In other words, the cameraman need rarely worry about focusing; the picture is practically speaking always in focus.

The manufacturer generally supplies with the camera a chart showing the forward and backward limits of sharpness for different lens stops. In the absence of these precise figures the above table is generally near enough (see also p. 16).

For the beginner, in filming children, and generally to simplify filming, the fixed focus lens is most useful. It gives perfectly sharp pictures in black-and-white. On the other hand, this type of lens rarely works at apertures larger than about f 2.5.

Note: When supplementary lenses are used to film close-ups, or an afocal system (such as the Hyper-Cinor, p. 20) for use in making titles, these tables and the usual rules are not applicable. In such cases, you must use the figures given by the manufacturer for the various supplementary lenses.

Focusing Lenses

All wide-aperture lenses, of f 1.9 to f 1.5, are mounted in focusing mounts—that is to say, they must be focused according to the distance of the subject. On these lenses there is a ring with a number of figures, representing these distances from infinity to a couple of feet.

In practice, it is not necessary to focus very exactly, except when you are working at a large aperture, say f 2.8 or larger. When the light permits working at say f 4, the zone of sharpness will extend from infinity down to 5 feet from the camera.

In other words, you can even use a focusing lens as if it were a fixed-focus one.

On the focusing ring of some lenses the figure 10 (the point of focus for 10 feet), or on Continental lenses 3, indicating 3 metres, is marked in red (if it is not, you can easily mark it yourself). One of the figures of the iris ring, generally the 4, is also in red, or sometimes there is an arrow opposite this figure. So at f 4 or smaller you can leave the focus ring set at 10 feet (or 3 metres), when everything will be sharp up to within 5 feet of the camera.

With the focusing lens used in this manner, supplementary lenses or the Hyper-Cinor system can still be used for close-ups. But you must focus accurately if you use the camera lens by itself for extreme close-ups.

Depth of Field

The lens iris also serves to vary the depth of field of the lens at close-up distances. As the iris is closed, so the zone of sharp focus is deepened, both in front of and behind the subject. At an aperture of f 4, if the lens is set to 10 feet, everything over 5 feet from the camera will be in focus.

On the other hand, working at f 1.9, which may be neces-

15

DEPTH OF FIELD OF ½ INCH (12.5 mm.) LENSES

Focused on (Feet)		Depth (Feet and Inches) at Aperture f					
		1.5	2	3.5	5.6	8	11
1	from	0–11½	0–11½	0–11	0–10½	0–10	0–9½
	to	1–0½	1–0½	1–1	1–2	1–3	1–5
2	from	1–10½	1–10	1–8½	1–7	1–5	1–3½
	to	2–2	2–3	2–5	2–9	3–4	3–7
3	from	2–9	2–7	2–5	2–2	1–10½	1–8
	to	3–4	3–6	4–0	5–0	7–6	15–0
5	from	4–3	4–0	3–6	3–0	2–6	2–1
	to	6–1	6–7	8–6	15–0	∞	∞
7	from	5–7	5–3	4–5	3–7	2–11	2–5
	to	9–4	10–6	17–0	∞	∞	∞
10	from	7–4	6–9	5–5	4–3	3–4	2–9
	to	15–6	23–0	∞	∞	∞	∞
15	from	8–2	8–6	6–8	5–0	3–9	3–0
	to	32–0	∞	∞	∞	∞	∞
∞	from	15–0	21–0	12–0	7–6	5–3	3–9
	to	∞	∞	∞	∞	∞	∞

DEPTH OF FIELD OF 1 INCH (25 mm.) LENSES

Focused on (Feet)		Depth (Feet and Inches) at Aperture f							
		1.5	2	2.8	4	5.6	8	11	16
3	from	2–11	2–11	2–10	2–9	2–8	2–7	2–6	2–4
	to	3–1	3–1	3–2	3–3	3–4	3–6	3–9	4–3
4	from	3–10	3–10	3–9	3–8	3–6	3–4	3–2	2–11
	to	4–2	4–2	4–4	4–5	4–6	5–0	5–8	6–7
5	from	4–10	4–9	4–7	4–6	4–4	4–0	3–7	3–3
	to	5–3	5–4	5–6	5–8	6–0	6–8	7–8	9–10
7	from	6–7	6–6	6–3	6–0	5–8	5–3	4–8	4–1
	to	7–6	7–8	7–11	8–5	9–0	10–0	14–0	23–0
10	from	9–3	8–11	8–7	8–0	7–6	6–6	5–10	5–2
	to	10–11	11–4	12–0	13–1	15–0	20–0	35–0	∞
15	from	13–4	12–9	12–0	11–0	10–0	8–6	7–6	6–0
	to	17–2	18–4	20–0	23–4	30–0	60–0	∞	∞
25	from	20–8	19–4	17–9	15–8	13–8	11–5	9–6	7–6
	to	31–6	35–6	43–0	51–6	∞	∞	∞	∞
∞	from	120	84–0	60–0	42–0	30–0	21–0	15–0	10–6
	to	∞	∞	∞	∞	∞	∞	∞	∞

16

DEPTH OF FIELD OF 1½ INCH (38 mm.) LENSES

Focused on (Feet)		Depth (Feet and Inches) at Aperture f						
		2	2.8	4	5.6	8	11	16
3	from	2–11	2–11	2–11	2–7	2–10	2–9	2–8
	to	3–1	3–1	3–1	3–2	3–3	3–4	3–5
4	from	3–11	3–11	3–10	3–9	3–8	3–7	3–5
	to	4–1	4–2	4–2	4–3	4–4	4–6	4–10
5	from	4–11	4–10	4–9	4–8	4–6	4–4	4–2
	to	5–2	5–3	5–4	5–5	5–7	5–10	6–4
7	from	6–9	6–8	6–6	6–4	6–1	5–10	5–5
	to	7–3	7–5	7–7	8–1	8–5	8–10	10–0
10	from	9–7	9–5	9–1	8–9	8–3	7–9	7–0
	to	10–6	10–10	11–2	11–9	12–9	14–3	17–6
15	from	13–11	13–6	13–0	12–3	11–5	10–4	9–2
	to	16–3	16–10	17–10	19–3	22–0	27–3	41–6
25	from	22–0	21–0	20–0	18–4	16–4	14–4	12–1
	to	28–9	30–9	34–0	40–0	53–6	∞	∞
∞	from	190	135	95–0	67–0	47–0	33–6	23–6
	to	∞	∞	∞	∞	∞	∞	∞

DEPTH OF FIELD OF 2 INCH (50 mm.) LENSES

Focused on (Feet)		Depth (Feet and Inches) at Aperture f						
		2.8	4	5.6	8	11	16	22
3	from	2–1	2–11	2–11	2–11	2–10	2–9	2–8
	to	3–1	3–1	3–1	3–2	3–2	3–4	3–4
4	from	3–11	3–11	3–10	3–10	3–9	3–8	3–6
	to	4–1	4–2	4–2	4–2	4–4	4–4	4–6
5	from	4–11	4–10	4–10	4–9	4–7	4–6	4–4
	to	5–2	5–2	5–3	5–4	5–6	5–8	6–0
7	from	6–10	6–9	6–7	6–6	6–3	6–0	5–8
	to	7–3	7–4	7–6	7–8	7–11	8–5	9–0
10	from	9–7	9–5	9–3	8–11	8–7	8–0	7–6
	to	10–6	10–8	10–11	11–4	12–0	13–1	15–0
15	from	14–1	13–9	13–4	12–9	12–0	11–0	10–0
	to	16–0	16–6	17–2	18–4	20–0	23–4	30–0
25	from	22–8	21–9	20–8	19–4	17–9	15–8	13–8
	to	28–0	29–6	31–6	35–6	43–0	61–0	∞
50	from	41–3	38–3	35–0	31–3	27–3	23–0	18–9
	to	63–6	72–0	84–6	124	∞	∞	∞
∞	from	240	165	120	84–0	60–0	42–0	30–0
	to	∞	∞	∞	∞	∞	∞	∞

17

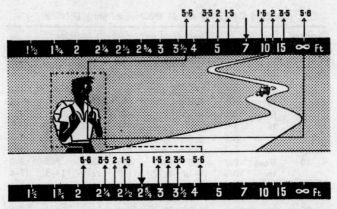

Most cine lenses carry a depth of field scale which moves past the distance scale during focusing, and shows the zone of sharp focus at any distance. The sharp zone always extends from the left-hand index mark of the aperture chosen to the corresponding right-hand index mark. Thus with the lens focused on 7 feet, the depth of field ranges from approximately 3¾ feet to infinity at *f* 5.6, or from just under 6 to somewhat over 9 feet at *f* 1.5. At close distances, the actual depth is less; thus at a distance of 2¾ feet and aperture *f* 5.6, the total depth is only about 2 feet—from just over 2 to over 4 feet.

sary in bad lighting conditions, and focusing on a close-up, for instance 4 feet or 5 feet, things will be sharp only between 4 feet and 7 feet.

From these two examples it will be clear that when the iris is stopped down the amount of light entering the camera is reduced, but the depth of field is increased.

The depth of field tables on p. 16 give complete figures for the zones of sharp focus for any distance and aperture.

Some lenses for cine cameras have depth of field scales engraved actually on the lens mount. On certain lenses an

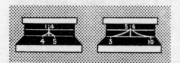

On some lenses the depth indicator takes the form of a curve of the lens barrel. By setting smaller apertures, a larger section of the curve appears.

18

automatic depth of field indicator is provided. For given settings of distance and aperture, coloured dots or the ends of two curves show the limits of the depth of field.

Coated Lenses

Practically every modern lens is "bloomed" or treated with an anti-reflection coating. Blooming reduces reflection of the rays of light entering the lens; it gives a crisper, sharper image, and increases slightly the amount of light passed by the lens, because reflection losses are largely eliminated. A bloomed lens has a peculiar purplish sheen.

With a pre-war lens, it may be possible to have it bloomed.

The Lens Mount

There are various types of lens mounts. The lens may be permanently mounted on the camera, or it may be fitted in an interchangeable mount.

Fixed mounting is extremely rare, and is used only on cheaper cameras. The lens is fixed permanently to the body of the camera, and cannot be removed with the object of using other lenses.

Lenses in fixed mounts are usually fixed-focus ones, and this restricts the possibilities of the camera—for instance, you cannot fit alternative lenses (pp. 20, 21).

A few expensive cameras are fitted with non-interchangeable lenses. In these cases it is the coupling between the irises of the lenses and of the built-in exposure meter which prevents the use of interchangeable mounting.

The Hyper-Cinor and the Ampli-Cinor can be fitted to these lenses to vary the field of view.

A standard interchangeable mount is used by the majority of manufacturers. The lens screws into the body of the camera and can easily be unscrewed, so that you can replace the normal lens by a longer or shorter focus lens.

There are, however, several varieties of interchangeable mount. To buy extra lenses you normally have to get in touch with the manufacturers.

19

Interchangeable Lenses

We have seen that the focal length determines the image angle and the scale of the picture (p. 12). With a range of lenses of different focal lengths we can therefore take in narrow or wide views, obtaining the effect of close-ups or long shots, all from one viewpoint. That is useful where we cannot get near enough to the subject for a close view, or when we cannot move back sufficiently to include all of it.

Wide-angle Lenses

Wide-angle lenses have a shorter focal length than the normal lens. For 8 mm. cameras this is usually about ⅜ inch or 9 mm., though ¼ inch or 6 mm. lenses are known. They are very rare, and cannot be used on many cameras because the construction of the mounting prevents the lens from being brought close enough to the film.

A special wide-angle attachment, the Hyper-Cinor, is available to enlarge the camera angle and double the field covered by the normal ½ inch lens. This attachment fits on to a normal lens; it has no iris, but simply a focusing ring. It does not affect the aperture of the normal lens, the diaphragm of which is still used.

For focusing, the normal lens must be set at infinity, except for close-ups.

In addition to wide-angle views, the attachment is equally suitable for titles, and generally for all close-up work.

The enlarged field given by the wide-angle attachment is shown in the viewfinder by means of a diverging lens which can be slipped into position. If this correction is not provided, a universal type of viewfinder must be mounted on the camera.

In close ups, beware of parallax errors (p. 26).

The various models of wide-angle attachments cannot be used on all types of lenses; the camera makers should be consulted as to the type to choose.

The front lens of the Hyper-Cinor is rather exposed, and

it is necessary to use an effective lens hood. This must be of a special type, otherwise there is a risk of cutting the field of the lens, or of vignetting the corners.

An alternative to the use of a wide-angle lens or attachment is to cover the field by panning the camera (p. 107).

Long-focus and Telephoto Lenses

Long-focus lenses have two, three or four times the normal focal length, giving a linear enlargement of two, three, or four times. We get the same effect as if we were looking through binoculars. Conversely, the field covered by such a lens is one-quarter, one-ninth, or one-sixteenth the area covered by the normal $\frac{1}{2}$ inch lens.

Long-focus lenses are useful for filming distant objects, when one cannot get close to them: sporting events, details

Some cameras have a lens turret which will take three lenses (p. 24). In this way we can use the wide-angle lens for medium shots, the standard lens for close-ups, and the long-focus lens for large close-ups, all from the same camera position. Changing over from one lens to the other then is a matter of seconds.

of scenery, architectural features, and in short everything of which a close-up view would be of interest to show the details.

As with normal lenses, various types of mounts are used. The screw type mount is most general, but unfortunately there is a variety of threads.

Some cameras need an adapter ring, which can generally be supplied by the manufacturers.

All long-focus lenses have an adjustable aperture and focus. Fixed-focus is not practical with lenses of longer focal length than normal.

To ensure a perfectly sharp image, the focusing must be adjusted very precisely, and a range-finder should be used.

A long-focus lens should be included in every film maker's kit. In the majority of cases a 1 inch (25 mm.) lens, yielding a magnification of 2 times, is sufficient.

Use a tripod whenever possible. The tripod must be very steady, otherwise the picture will jitter on the screen.

Long-focus lenses giving a magnification of three times (focal length 1½ inches or 38 mm.) can be very useful, for instance in filming sporting events, races, etc. With lenses of still longer focal length a heavy rock-steady cine tripod is absolutely essential. Moreover, even motor vibration may cause camera shake.

An optical viewfinder giving a clear and sufficiently large image is desirable to permit accurate framing of the picture.

When buying a long-focus lens, always state for what type of camera it is intended. The standardisation of such equipment leaves much to be desired. It is often advisable to return the camera to the manufacturers with the new lens, so that the setting can be correctly adjusted and fixed.

Variable Focus Lenses

Instead of using different lenses for the various focal lengths, it is often an advantage to use a single lens of variable focus.

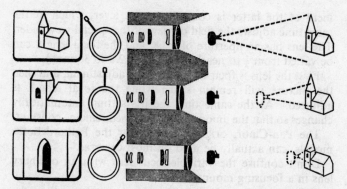

With a variable focus lens the movement of a lever changes the focal length by altering the lens separation. This can take place during shooting, and thus gradually narrow down the angle of view from wide-angle long shots (*top*) to telephoto close-ups (*bottom*); the effect is similar to shots obtained by tracking.

The Pan-Cinor variable focus lens enables the field of view to be varied continuously, the effect ranging from that of a normal lens to that of a long-focus lens.

All sorts of special effects can be achieved without the use of a camera truck, for example, the zoom effect of the camera approaching or receding from the subject, and the effect of the camera moving with the subject.

The lens consists of fixed and movable elements; move-

The control of the variable focus lens is a lever which may move forward and back or rotate round the mount. The movement is coupled to a similar system in the viewfinder which thus always shows the correct view.

23

ment of the latter is controlled by a lever, which at the same time adjusts the field of view of the special viewfinder. The lens has an aperture of f 2.8, and the focal length can be varied from $\frac{1}{2}$ to nearly $1\frac{1}{2}$ inches (12.5 to 36 mm.).

First the lens is focused by the front adjustment, and then the picture will remain sharp while the focal length is adjusted. At the same time the iris setting automatically changes so that the amount of light passed remains constant.

The Pan-Cinor, originally made for the Paillard-Bolex models, can actually be used on most cameras.

Don't confuse the variable-focus lens with an ordinary lens in a focusing mount.

Lens Turrets

So that you can switch rapidly from one lens to another, some cameras are fitted with a lens turret. On the front of the camera is a disc, which carries up to three lenses.

Various combinations of lenses can be mounted on the turret. For instance, we can have a lens of normal focus, one of rather longer focus such as 23 mm. (just under 1 inch), and another of longer focus still, say 35 mm. ($1\frac{3}{8}$ inches).

Alternatively, fit a normal focus lens, another of the same focus but with a wide-angle attachment, and a long-focus lens of 23 mm. or 35 mm.

On some cameras two lenses, one of normal focus and the other of longer focus, are mounted on a sliding panel in front of the taking aperture. This arrangement permits the use of a coupled exposure meter (p. 80) which is connected to the lens iris.

Another version of turret has the two lenses of normal and long focus mounted on a panel which is pivoted on its centre, and carries the front portion of a viewfinder for each lens. This arrangement saves masking the viewfinder field and gives the full field of each lens, clearly and automatically. Certain three-lens turrets also incorporate a viewfinder for each lens.

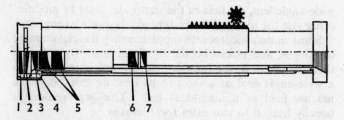

Some universal finders work on a principle similar to variable focus lenses. The fixed part of the optical system consists of two prism wedges 1 and 2, the framing aperture 4, and the lenses 3 and 5. The movable section carries the eyepiece lenses 6 and 7. This finder covers a range of focal lengths from $\frac{1}{4}$ to 3 inches.

Viewfinders

The viewfinder should give a clear, sharp image, the right way up, showing exactly what will be recorded on the film. The commonest type of finder is the optical one, and is based on the principle of the Galilean telescope.

On the front lens (that nearer the camera lens) there is often a tiny black cross right in the centre of the field, to facilitate centring. Sometimes, too, there may be one or two lines, one above the other, indicating the limits of the frame in filming close-ups. This parallax correction is necessary when filming nearer than 5 feet or so. At such close range the finder, as it is in a slightly different position from the lens, does not show the exact view recorded on the film (p. 26).

In one camera which has a coupled exposure meter, a little cross in the centre of the viewfinder field shows the point at which the needle of the meter must be set.

In the viewfinder of some cameras an arrow pops up when the 25 feet of film have been run through. This arrow is the signal to stop taking, but the motor must be kept running to run off the protecting leader.

Sometimes the footage can be read in the finder.

When the normal lens is changed for a long-focus or

wide-angle lens, the field of the viewfinder must be modified otherwise the limits of the picture will be quite wrong.

Some finders incorporate supplementary lenses, mounted on hinges, and placed behind the front lens. By swinging them in position, the normal field of view is increased to a wide-angle field of a short-focus lens, or reduced to the narrow field of a long-focus lens. This arrangement is usually limited to two extra focal lengths.

Alternatively, the finder may incorporate two hinged masks to provide respectively the fields for 2 times and 3 times long-focus lenses.

If a wide-angle lens or attachment is used with such a camera, the new field of view is given by means of an additional element, fixed to the front of the finder.

Cameras with lenses on a turret or two-lens panel sometimes carry alternative front elements to the finder on the turret panel.

Strictly speaking, the term universal viewfinder should be reserved for those finders which fit on to the camera, in the position intended by the maker. They should provide, in addition to parallax correction, an adjustment giving all the different fields covered by the usual range of lenses, from the wide-angle field up to the field of 1, 1½, and 2 inch lenses.

Parallax Correction

The finder should ideally show the exact picture which will be photographed on the film. In practice, this is not always the case.

If you look at the front of your camera, you will see that the viewfinder is necessarily in a different position from the taking lens. There are several possible arrangements:

Finder above taking lens. If you film a subject in close-up —say 3 feet from the lens—and you do not want to cut off part of the subject, you must leave a bit more headroom above the subject in the finder. Several types of finder have a marking showing the top limit of the frame.

26

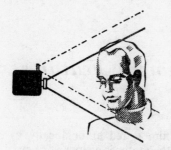
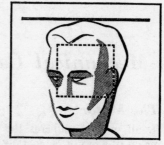

As the viewpoint of the finder is slightly higher than that of the camera lens, the latter includes less of the top of the subject (*left*). Allow for that when taking close-ups. Some finders indicate this parallax correction by a line in the finder field (*right*) and may also include a frame (dotted) to show the view with a long-focus lens.

Finder to the left of taking lens (looking at the front of the camera). A double correction is necessary for close-ups: first, the same correction as before, leaving more headroom above the subject; secondly, place the subject more to the left in the finder.

Finder level with taking lens but to right (looking at the front of the camera). In this case, you have to place the subject more to the right in the finder.

The back lens or eyepiece of such finders often carries a separate parallax adjustment. This works by displacing the eyepiece, swinging round the optical axis of the finder, and gives accurately the limits of the picture for close-ups. This adjustment should be made for all shots taken at less than 3 feet distance.

Sometimes an adjustment is also provided to focus the viewfinder to the user's eyesight.

Generally there is no need to worry about parallax except at short distances. The exact distance at which allowance must be made will depend upon the actual job.

When the correction is made mechanically, by offsetting the eyepiece, do not forget to re-centre it immediately after shooting, or subsequent scenes may be out of the centre.

27

Mechanical Camera Features

The Motor

IN all modern cameras the film is fed automatically by means of a motor. Generally the motor is a clockwork one, wound either by a handle or a key. The motor gives always the one speed of 16 frames per second, and often other speeds, the uses of which we will consider later.

It is always advisable to wind the motor fully before starting a shooting session; it is equally advisable to give the key a few turns between scenes. Some cameras have a comparatively small motor, which will run for only about 20 seconds at normal speed, and it is then necessary to rewind after every scene.

In at least two cameras the clockwork motor is replaced by a small electric motor, fed from a $4\frac{1}{2}$ volt battery, not only to ensure a constant speed but also to run a reasonable footage of film without changing the battery. A good-quality battery will run at least five to seven double-eight films at normal speed.

In some cameras the spring motor can be uncoupled and replaced by an ordinary electric motor. Such a motor may be fed either from the mains or from accumulators.

Filming Speeds

Most modern 8 mm. cameras, other than the simplest models, provide a range of running speeds. The most usual are 8, 16, 24 and 32 frames per second. More expensive cameras can also run at 64 frames, to produce slow-motion effects (p. 29).

The normal speed of 16 frames per second is the minimum

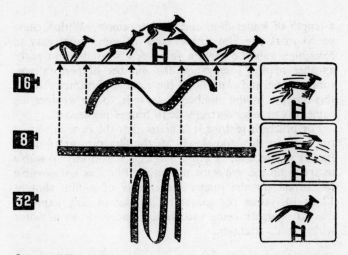

By using different filming speeds we can retard or speed up the action on the screen. At 8 frames per second a given length of film covers twice as long a time of the action as at the standard 16 f.p.s. Consequently the movement will seem much faster when projected at standard speed. At 32 f.p.s. the same length of film covers only half as much time and the action is slowed down by being "expanded" on projection.

necessary in projection to provide normal reproduction of movement on the screen. During one second 16 frames are recorded, with the uniform exposure time of $\frac{1}{30}$ to $\frac{1}{32}$ second for each frame. In a few cameras the exposure time is rather shorter—possibly $\frac{1}{40}$ or even $\frac{1}{50}$ second—but generally one is safe in reckoning on an exposure time of $\frac{1}{30}$ second when setting the iris by an exposure meter.

This exposure of about $\frac{1}{30}$ second applies only when the motor is fully up to speed. If the camera is fitted with a single-picture device, the exposure time is not $\frac{1}{30}$ second, but generally much longer—$\frac{1}{15}$ or even $\frac{1}{10}$ second—because of the inertia in starting up each frame. This inertia is also the cause of over-exposed frames at the start of scenes.

It is wise, at least once a year, to check the accuracy of the motor at normal speed. The check can be made with a length of leader film, and is quite simple. With a china pencil mark the film with a cross at some point easy to recognise, run the camera for a few seconds, and make another mark. Then count the number of perforations, subtract one, and you will get the number of frames. Divide this number by the number of seconds, to see whether the camera is running correctly at 16 frames per second.

For practical reasons it is better that the camera should run too fast than too slowly. If the film runs at 18 or 20 frames per second, as often happens, it is always possible to speed up the projector to match. But it is not possible to correct for the jumpy movements of a film shot at 12 or 14 frames per second. This occasionally happens, due to chargers being incorrectly loaded or to a motor which needs attention.

Slow Speeds

The slow speed on a cine camera may be 8 or 12 frames per second. The exposure time is longer—about $\frac{1}{16}$ or $\frac{1}{25}$ second respectively.

The slow speed is suitable for titles, trick work, and occasionally in poor light, when there is no movement in the picture.

A person moving normally but filmed at this speed will give a ludicrous effect on projection. Everybody will appear to rush about twice as fast as usually. If in exceptional cases it should be necessary to use the 8-frame speed, everybody in the picture should be told to avoid any rapid movement. The slow speed is, however, useful for intentionally comic results.

Fast Speeds

Running the camera at a faster speed than the film is going to be projected slows down the action on the screen. If the camera speed is high enough, a fast movement can be made to look quite leisurely; this is in fact slow-motion.

In filming people in rapid motion, moving vehicles (although this is rarely advisable), the speed of 24 frames is useful. The exposure time at this speed is about $\frac{1}{50}$ second.

This speed may also be used in panning (p. 108) to avoid a blurred picture due to camera movement.

Incidentally, if you intend adding a magnetic sound track to your film, the speed of 24 frames per second—that used in the professional cinema—will give a better sound quality in reproduction. Naturally you must make sure that your projector is capable of running at this speed, too.

The higher speed of 32 frames per second (corresponding exposure time $\frac{1}{65}$ second) gives a partial slow-motion effect, and can be used when the camera does not provide a 64-frame speed, or when the light is insufficient for it. It is suitable, too, for subjects in rapid motion, moving vehicles, etc.

It is important that the camera should not be run without film at this speed—there is a risk of the motor over-shooting at the end of its run, causing damage.

The true slow-motion effect is obtained only at 64 frames per second.

Never run the camera empty at this speed.

Before shooting, wind the motor fully, but never let the motor run right down at 64 frames per second; four or five seconds is enough for quite a long scene.

Single Frame Shooting

When the camera is set to expose single frames, each pressure on the starting button exposes one frame of film. This refinement is used chiefly for titles, trick work, and occasionally for a speeded-up (time-lapse) effect—for example, the growth of plants.

Rather than attempt to check the exposure time on single-frame setting, it is wiser to rely upon the manufacturers' information; generally it is about $\frac{1}{20}$ or $\frac{1}{15}$ second.

To avoid any risk of camera shake, it is advisable to drive the camera through a flexible coupling, where a suitable fitting is provided on the camera. On one camera the single-frame setting runs with a constant shutter opening, or with a longer exposure period corresponding to the "B" setting of a photographic shutter.

Reverse Action

On some cameras a reverse drive is fitted. It is of obvious value for trick work (p. 123), but all too often it is the cause of film jams!

The camera is always driven backwards by hand, through an extra handle, and never from the motor. Different cameras have different mechanisms.

On one model the motor is declutched and an extra handle drives directly to the film feeding mechanism. The feed spool takes up and the footage counter counts backwards. Since the motor is declutched, it is possible to run a whole film, whatever its length.

On all other cameras with which reverse drive is possible its use is restricted by the fact that the motor remains coupled, and the driving handle has in effect to wind up the spring. Obviously you must first be sure that the motor is almost completely run down before a reverse action shot of any length is undertaken.

Another difficulty is the inertia of the feed spool. If this takes up when the camera is run backwards, there is no risk of a hold-up. But if it has no reverse drive, only a very short length of film can be turned backwards—for example, just sufficient for a dissolve—otherwise the camera will jam, and you will find the film has wrapped itself in accordion pleats!

When running the camera backwards, always put the cap on the lens (except when you are exposing backwards for trick work), otherwise the shutter will continue to expose the film.

Dissolves

The reverse drive is used chiefly to produce dissolves. That is, one scene fades into another. This is done as follows:

1. End the first scene with a simple fade-out—that is to say, close the iris during the last few inches of film.

2. Put the cap on the lens and wind the film back for a length about equal to that during which you were closing the iris.

3. Remove the lens cap, and with the diaphragm almost closed, start shooting the next scene. Slowly open the iris up to the stop required for that scene. Then, if there has been no hold-up due to the rewinding of the film, carry on shooting the second scene.

In practice the effect of a dissolve is to some extent neutralised by the corrections automatically made during processing of the film. During the second exposure which forms part of the processing, any scenes which are under-exposed receive a compensating exposure. This compensation system, although it may not be always desirable, is generally very valuable, because it increases the exposure latitude (p. 62) and saves many a wrongly exposed scene.

Frame and Footage Counters

So that you can see at any moment how much film you have exposed, and how much is left, one or two footage counters are provided.

The simplest is the lever-type indicator. A lever rests on the film, and the thickness of the layers of the film indicates the footage on the spool. This arrangement is not particularly accurate and the reading depends upon whether the film is tightly wound in its original winding, or whether it has been loosely rewound after the second run. However, it does provide an automatic indication of whether or not there is any film in the gate. The driven counter is more accurate, but necessitates an adjustment when the film is

33

changed over to the second run. When the film is inserted in the camera, run it for a few seconds to ensure that it is properly loaded. Then close the door and set the counter at the start mark. At this stage there is still some of the leader film to be unwound and the usable part of the film has not reached the gate. When the counter reaches its zero point you can start exposing. This job of loading and unloading should always be carried out in a dim light.

Some types of automatic counter set themselves automatically to the start mark when the door of the camera is opened. When the film is in position, run the motor until the counter reaches zero.

At the end of the film—that is to say, at the end of the usable portion—when the counter indicates a length of 25 feet (or 50 or 100 feet, according to the load), stop shooting. Do not yet open the camera; the trailer at the end must be run through. You cannot mistake this point, because the noise of the motor will change, since there is no longer any film in the gate.

On some cameras an audible signal at set intervals indicates the length of film run off. This device does not take the place of the footage counter, which is found on all cameras.

Frame counters are an additional feature on certain high-class cameras. They show the actual number of frames filmed (usually on dials reading units and hundreds) and are very useful for single-picture and reverse-action work.

The Film Feeding System

Raw stock for 8 mm. cameras is supplied either on a spool, with leader at the beginning and end of the film, or in a charger or magazine. But, whichever way the film is protected, it must be fed regularly behind the lens by suitable mechanism.

If you take out the lens you will find a rectangular aperture, behind which a shutter prevents you seeing any

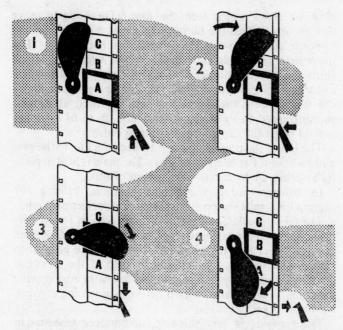

The film transport consists of one or more claws synchronized with the shutter. The latter covers the film aperture or gate while the claw pulls the film down by one frame, and uncovers the film again for about 1/30 second while the claw returns to its original position. This cycle takes place 16 times per second when the camera runs at standard speed.

farther. If you press the starting button, the motor will run and the shutter will periodically open and shut; when it is open you can look right through to the film. This cycle of events occurs all the time the button is pressed.

Now look inside the camera, and you will see the gate in which the film is held flat by a pressure plate. In the gate, just behind the lens, is a rectangular aperture or window, which must be kept scrupulously clean—the slightest trace of dirt here will be photographed on every frame of film.

Just below this aperture and to one side you will see the

claw or claws which feed the film. These claws move downwards to feed the film one frame at a time (or in the opposite direction when the camera runs backwards). The movement of the claws is synchronized with that of the shutter; while the shutter is closed the claws feed the film a distance of one frame, then the shutter opens, exposing the film. These two operations are repeated at normal running speed 16 times per second, and up to 64 times per second when the camera runs at top speed.

The job of the pressure plate is to keep the film in the gate and to hold it flat behind the lens. The plate is held in place by a spring, or by means of a system of links.

In cameras using single-eight chargers, closing the camera door puts the pressure plate in its correct position.

The feed sprocket, a drum with four teeth, is found only in the more costly cameras. Its job is to help the film from the feed spool into the gate, and then from the gate on to the take-up spool. After leaving the top of the sprocket, the film forms a loop before entering the gate; after leaving the gate, it forms another loop before again being engaged by the sprocket.

The sprocket is very valuable, and indeed essential in cameras running at 64 frames per second. The film must be threaded on it very carefully.

In some cameras there is no sprocket, yet the loops are maintained top and bottom of the gate. Sometimes the film passes round stationary rollers, or a rubber-covered roller is driven from the motor.

The majority of camera faults are due to the pressure plate. It should be carefully examined when a camera is purchased. It must be in the correct position when the camera is loaded.

Due to vibration (for example, in transit), the pressure plate may get out of place, and allow the film to run continuously through the gate without producing any trace of a visible image. This trouble is rarely found with automatically located pressure plates.

Types of 8 mm. Cameras

THE cameras available to the 8 mm. user may be divided into three main types, according to their general construction, their mechanical devices, and the consequent advantages in use.

To simplify reference to, and comparison of, the various camera features, the camera diagrams throughout this chapter are lettered, as far as applicable, according to a standard system as follows.

Lens and focusing controls

L1—Standard lens.
L2—Alternative lenses or spaces for them.
L3—Lens turret.
L4—Lens mount.
L5—Aperture scale.
L6—Aperture control.
L7—Focusing scale.

Viewfinder features

V1—Viewfinder.
V2—Finder eyepiece.
V3—Parallax correction.
V4—Focal length adjustment for various lenses.

Mechanism controls

M1—Starter button.
M2—Safety catch.
M3—Speed control.
M4—Winding key or handle.
M5—Footage counter.
M6—Footage counter re-setting knob.
M7—Frame counter.
M8—Continuous running lock.
M9—Single frame control.
M10—Driving handle (hand drive)

Other outside features

O1—Depth of field table.
O2—Exposure calculator or table.
O3—Carrying handle.
O4—Tripod bush.

Film path and transport

F1—Film.
F2—Transport mechanism.
F3—Charger or magazine.
F4—Gate.
F5—Pressure plate.
F6—Pressure plate adjustment.
F7—Loop former.
F8—Feed spindle.
F9—Feed spool.
F10—Take-up spindle.
F11—Take-up spool.
F12—Guide roller.
F13—Sprocket.
F14—Top loop.
F15—Bottom loop.
F16—Lever of footage counter.

Special features

These are numbered from **S1** onwards and vary from camera to camera, being explained in the appropriate caption.

Simple Cameras

Under this heading we will include cameras with the devices necessary for filming, but without additional technical refinements.

They usually run at a fixed speed of 16 frames per second, with sometimes a single-picture device.

The lens is generally of good quality. In the lower-priced cameras it will be in a fixed-focus mount—working generally at f 2.5. The lens will be of the triplet type (consisting of three elements) and bloomed. However, it does not always have the necessary correction for colour. Because of this, the projected picture may lack sharpness and detail.

Sometimes a better lens with a larger aperture of f 1.9 is fitted, usually in an interchangeable focusing mount.

Most simple cameras have an optical viewfinder. The front lens is sometimes engraved with one or more squares, which indicate the fields of other lenses.

Parallax between the viewfinder and the taking lens must be allowed for in use, no compensation being provided.

The majority of cameras, even those of moderate price, have a mechanical footage counter driven from the motor; this type of counter is more accurate than the system using a roller riding on the film on the feed spool, which gives only an approximate reading.

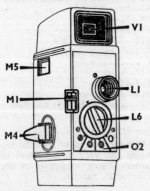

The American Bell & Howell 220 (and British B.G.—Bell & Howell 624) is a particularly simple camera with fixed focus lens, the cine equivalent of the snap-shooter's box. The viewfinder (**V1**) is extra large, and the aperture is controlled by a big key (**L6**) in conjunction with a simple exposure calculator (**O2**). For standard features see p. 37.

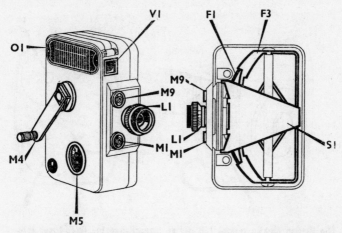

The German Blue Spot 8 mm. camera has a bloomed fixed-focus lens, and a single speed, while a second release button (**M9**) gives single-frame exposures. The plate (**S1**) keeps the charger in position and automatically releases the pressure plate. For standard features see p. 37.

The French Cinegel Reinette 8 camera has either a fixed-focus or a focusing Roussel lens. The speed control (**M3**) is really a brake which retards the spring motor and thus permits only speeds slower than 16 f.p.s. This is useful when shooting scenes with not much movement in poor light, as it yields more exposure. For standard features see p. 37.

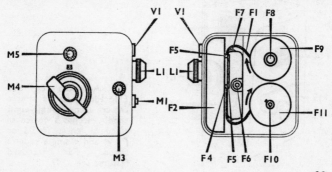

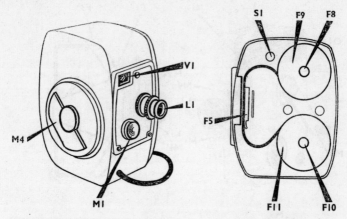

The British Dekko model 128 has an interchangeable fixed-focus lens and other lenses can be fitted for close-up and telephoto work. It has the minimum of controls necessary for successful filming. The film counter works by means of a measuring arm (**SI**) and indicates the end of the load by a signal in the viewfinder. An exposure guide is built-in and speeds up the process of calculating the aperture setting for correct exposures. For standard features see p. 37.

The gate and feed mechanism are generally similar in most simple cameras. Usually they use a 25 feet spool of film, although one camera in this class holds a 50 feet spool, and there are German cameras using a single-eight charger.

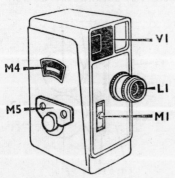

The American De Jur Eldorado is also a simple camera using double-eight spools. It has a device of standard lenses (f 2·5 or f 1·9) and a single camera speed. For standard features see p. 37.

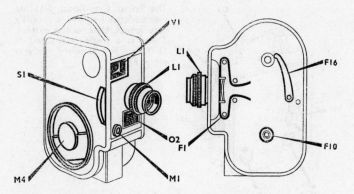

The French GIC-8 is fitted with an interchangeable *f* 1.9 lens. The view-finder incorporates a mask to reduce the field of view for long-focus lenses. This shows accurately the smaller field of view. The shutter casing (**S1**) projects a little outside the body on the right-hand side. To ensure a controlled loop, the film runs under and over four guide rollers. For standard features see p. 37.

The British and American Brownie camera is a specially simple model to handle, and has a fixed focus *f* 2·7 lens and a single speed of 16 f.p.s. loading is made easy by the absence of sprockets. The turret model incorporates a telephoto and a wide-angle attachment which can be brought in front of the built-in lens when required. For standard features see p. 37.

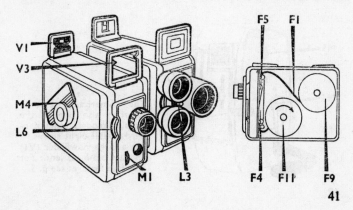

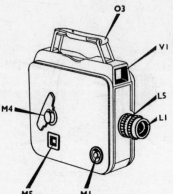

The British Cine-Kodak 8-55 has a fixed-focus lens and a specially easy sprocketless loading system. There is a single film speed of 16 f.p.s. For standard features see p. 37.

As these simple cameras have the essential requirements for filming, there is no reason why they should not produce perfect films provided they are accurately made. A lot depends on the optical system, and in particular on the accuracy of mounting of the lens in the camera. If the image is perfectly sharp, results will be excellent.

Naturally the motor should run at a constant speed. To prevent it losing its power, look after it carefully. A few turns of the key after every scene will keep the motor running at normal speed.

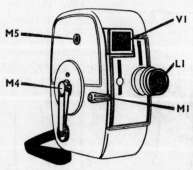

The American Keystone Capri is also one of the simpler models using standard double-eight spools. It has a large viewfinder (**VI**) and a fixed-focus lens. For standard features see p. 37.

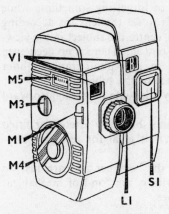

VI
M5
M3
MI
M4
LI
SI

The American Revere 55 incorporates an automatic iris fade control (**SI**) which comes into action at the beginning and end of each take, and is controlled by the starter lever. The Revere 50 is similar, but without fade control. Both cameras have a top speed of 64 f.p.s. For standard features see p. 37.

The type of camera using chargers is generally superior, for although such models are of quite simple design, they are very well built; they are, of course, more expensive.

Using a Simple Camera

If you cannot spend a lot of time on your hobby, it is best to choose a camera of this class, which has no unnecessary gadgets.

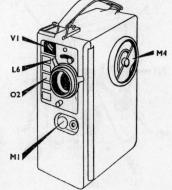

VI
L6
O2
M4
MI

The German 8 mm. Siemens camera features a fixed-focus lens which permits telephoto shots with the help of a special tele-attachment. For standard features see p. 37.

You will not run the risk of forgetting something while taking. All you have to do is to set the lens iris according to the brightness of the scene, centre the subject in the viewfinder, and press the starting button. There is no need even to worry, as you have to in still photography, about exposure time and the distance of the subject.

This type of camera is fully adequate for straightforward filming.

On the other hand, it cannot be easily altered or fitted with additional devices, nor is it ideal for technical film-making with tricks, etc.

It is the ideal camera for the beginner to learn his job with, and for the amateur who is not fond of mechanical complication and technicalities.

Cameras of Greater Scope

This is the type of camera you will choose if you want to make more advanced films. Here are some of its features.

The motor—the heart of the camera—is better made; it is heavier, quieter, and runs more smoothly and steadily. Besides the normal speed of 16 frames per second, this

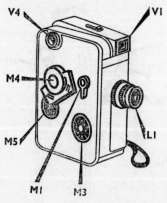

The American Ampro 340 has a precision viewfinder which is adjustable for lenses of different focal length. The motor has six speeds from 12 to 64 f.p.s. For standard features see p. 37.

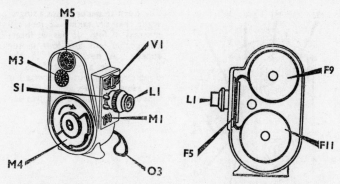

In the British Bell & Howell Sportster a locking ring (**S1**) permits rapid changing of lenses. The viewfinder includes masks to suit the different lenses. An exposure calculator is fitted in the camera body. The speeds range from 16 to 64 frames per second. For standard features see p. 37.

The Swiss Paillard Bolex C8 is a development of an earlier model, the L8, and has a number of advanced features. The film counter automatically returns to zero when the camera door is opened. An engraved curve (**S3**) shows the position and size of the loops required when loading. A cable release socket (**S1**) permits the use of a standard cable release. A table (**S2**) indicates the exposure times corresponding to various filming speeds. The lens is interchangeable and fitted in a standard mount.
A more advanced model of this camera, the Bolex B8, has two lenses mounted on a twin turret (p. 56). For standard features see p. 37.

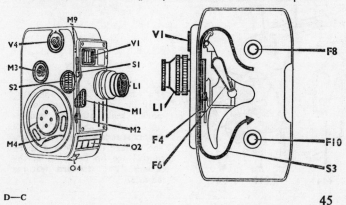

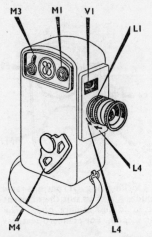

The German Bauer 8 uses a single-eight charger, taking 33 feet (10 metres) of film. It has an interchangeable lens and four motor speeds. A new model of the Bauer-8 uses a standard 25 ft. double-8 spool, but otherwise has the same features as the charger model. For standard features see p. 37.

class of camera has additional speeds: a low speed of 8 or 12 frames, and higher speeds such as 24, 32, and in some cameras 64 frames per second, the last for real slow-motion effects.

The single-frame drive is included, as well as reverse action. The latter facility is not altogether desirable, for it is sometimes the cause of the film jamming.

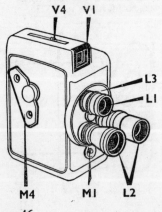

The American De Jur Spectator (available also as a single-lens model) takes standard double-eight spools, and has a range of camera speeds from 12 to 48 f.p.s. The footage indicator and speed control are on the back of the camera. For standard features see p. 37.

The American De Jur DH 100 (without turret) and DH 300 (with three-lens turret) take double-eight magazines.

An automatic fade control (SI) produces fades when required. The lenses are fitted in standard screw-in mounts. The viewfinder is adjustable for the different focal lengths available. For standard features see p. 37.

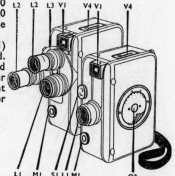

The lens is always of high quality, working at an aperture of *f* 1.9 or larger, and with bloomed surfaces. Focusing adjustment may go down to a couple of feet. The interchangeable mounting enables lenses of different focal lengths to be used. Some models have a lens turret.

An optical viewfinder is supplied by most manufacturers as standard equipment. By means of either masks or an optical system, the field is modified to suit long-focus lenses.

Sometimes additional devices are included. Some viewfinders indicate the end of the film or incorporate a footage counter. Usually there is some means of parallax correction.

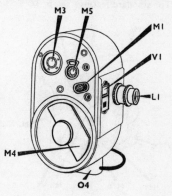

The British Dekko model 110 features a fixed-focus lens as its standard optical equipment, but will take other lenses as well. It has provision for single frame exposures as well as continuous runs, and for remote control. For standard features see p. 37.

47

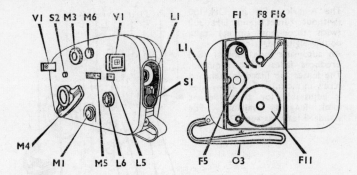

The Belgian Carena Geva-8 has the lens set in a protective housing. This housing serves a number of purposes. First, it protects the lens. It also provides the space for holding the built-in yellow and orange swing out filters (S1). Lastly, the housing acts as a built-in lens hood. The optical viewfinder (V1) retracts into the camera body and is released by the button (S2) for quick operation. It is also marked with engraved squares. For standard features see p. 37.

The French Ercsam has its lens fitted in a quick-change bayonet mount. The viewfinder is adjustable for wide-angle and long focus lenses, while the de luxe model has a universal finder with variable field. The viewfinder is also fitted with a parallax correcting mechanism. A special button (M8) serves as safety catch as well as continuous running lock. Single-frame and reverse drive controls are included for trick work. For standard features see p. 37.

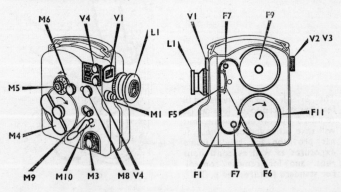

The American Keystone Magazine-8 takes double-eight magazines, the light traps of which are opened inside the camera by the button (S1). The Keystone K32 Olympic is very similar but takes double-eight spools. The lens is interchangeable and the speeds range from 8 to 64 f.p.s. For standard features see p. 37.

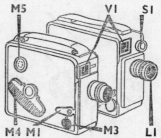

To be efficient this must be accurately made and adjusted actually on the camera.

With long-focus lenses the mask in the viewfinder gives quite a small image. A separate optical viewfinder may be used, giving a clearer image.

For accurate indication of the length of film exposed, and the length remaining to be exposed, a counter driven from the motor is the only satisfactory type. The system in which a roller rides on the film on the feed spool gives only approximate readings; this device may be the cause of jamming when the film is wound back for reverse-action.

Cameras of this second class show improvements also in the methods of loading and unloading. The threading of the film is much facilitated by the use of double-eight or single-eight chargers, and by an improved gate. The pressure on the pressure plate is evenly balanced and the plate fits freely in the gate channel.

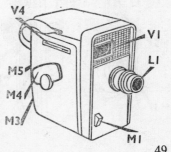

The American Kodak Medallion takes double-eight magazines. A film counter and speed control for 16 to 49 f.p.s. are located at the rear. The starting button (M1) also acts as single frame release. For standard features see p. 37.

49

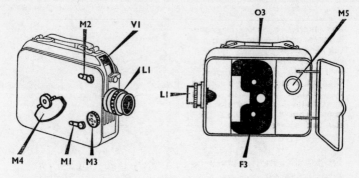

The American Cine-Kodak Magazine-8 is the prototype of popular-price double-eight charger-type cameras. The interchangeable lens is in a bayonet mount, while the finder is adjustable to the different fields of view. The charger (**F3**) is simply inserted in the camera, it incorporates its own transport mechanism and pressure plate, and the film needs no threading. For standard features see p. 37.

The Czechoslovakian Meopta Admira 8C features an interchangeable lens, a speed range from 10 to 64 f.p.s., as well as a single frame release, a socket for a cable release, and delayed action. An audible scene length indicator helps the cameraman to keep a check on his timing. For standard features see p. 37.

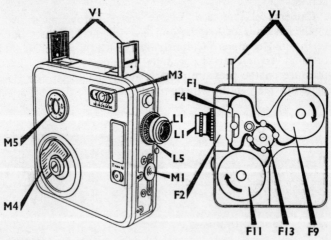

The British Miller is a spool-loading camera, has a range of motor speeds from 8 to 64 f.p.s., and an interchangeable focusing lens. The starter button can be used as a single-frame release. For standard features see p. 37.

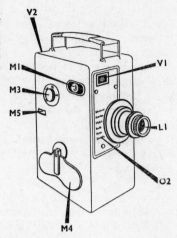

Utilizing the Increased Scope

This is the normal type of camera for the amateur to buy. Its price may be somewhat higher, but it is justified by the quality of results, the ease of handling, and the pleasure one derives from possessing such equipment.

The high-quality lens enables pictures to be taken in any

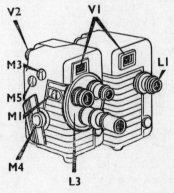

The American Revere B 61 is very compact, being just twice the size of the double-eight charger which it uses. It has an interchangeable lens, adjustable finder and five-speed motor. The Revere B 63 is substantially the same camera, but with a three-lens turret. For standard features see p. 37.

51

weather, or indoors with the minimum of lighting. The lens is colour-corrected, and gives a sharp image without fringing. The interchangeable mount enables long-focus lenses to be used.

The motor with its powerful spring gives a longer running time without winding, although it is advisable to give the key a few turns after every scene.

The range of speeds allows for working under varying conditions: the low speed for use when the light is too poor for working at normal speed, even with a lens aperture of f 1.9; or on the other hand, the high speeds for filming moving vehicles, or for real slow-motion at 64 f.p.s.

If you buy a camera of this type you will have a wide choice, but you should carefully weigh the pros and cons of the various models. In particular, consider the relative advantages and disadvantages of chargers and spools.

The American double-eight charger is very practical, but is not widely used. The single-eight charger also is far from universal.

Sooner or later you will complete your camera outfit by buying additional lenses. With this in mind, examine

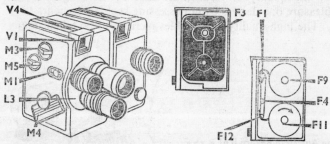

The American Revere 80 and the Wollensak 58 (which is substantially the same camera) take double-eight spools and have interchangeable lenses with a variable focus viewfinder. The turret models (Revere 84, Wollensak 53) have a three-lens turret. A similar range of models by Revere (40 and 44) and Wollensak (28 and 23 respectively) take double-eight magazines (the interior of both types is shown). The door lock is on the front with the magazine cameras, and on the side with the spool models.

52

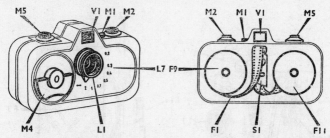

The German Zeiss Movikon-8 represents a departure from the traditional design of cine cameras and is held in the same way as a miniature still camera. The lens is consequently mounted in the side of the body. The film goes through two right angle twists on its path from the feed spool through the gate (where the loops are maintained by the plate **S1**) and on to the take-up spool. For standard features see p. 37.

the viewfinder carefully; some types of finder, fitted with masks for matching with long-focus lenses, give a very clear image although it is too small. Others give so poor an image even though it may be larger, that you will have to buy a better type of finder.

The focusing lens which can be adjusted to operate as a fixed focus lens has possibilities—for instance, for close-ups supplementary lenses can be used.

The American Bell & Howell Filmo Auto-8 incorporates an audible film counter, visual indication of each foot of film, and gives an audible warning 2 feet before the motor stops. A mask automatically obtsructs the finder when the film is finished. The lenses are mounted on a turret which also carries viewfinder lenses to change the field of view. For standard features see p. 37.

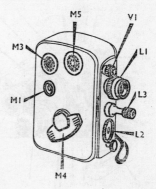

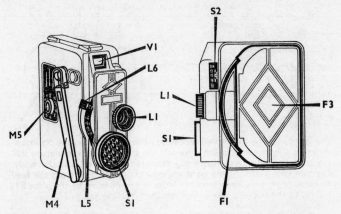

The important feature of the German Agfa Movex 8L is the built-in photo-electric exposure meter (**S1**) coupled to the lens aperture. The aperture setting, controlled by the lever (**L6**), is visible in the view-finder. Setting the scale (**S2**) allows for the speed of the film used. The Movex takes single-8 chargers (**F3**) holding 33 feet (10 metres) of film. For standard features see p. 37.

The French Emel C93 has a three-lens turret while a separate multiple finder with parallax correction shows the corresponding field of view. In addition to having speeds from 8 to 64 f.p.s. the motor also permits reverse shooting. Loading is simplified by a bracket (**S1**) which pulls back the pressure plate and frees the rollers (**F12**). For standard features see p. 37.

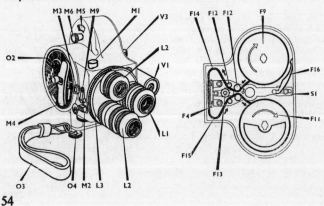

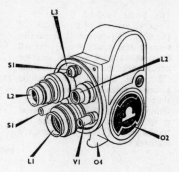

The British Bell & Howell Viceroy has a three-lens turret, again incorporating viewfinder front elements (**S1**) corresponding to the lenses used. For standard features see p. 37.

High-grade Cameras

In this class are cameras which contain all the refinements that mechanics, optics and the ingenuity of inventors can devise and fit into a tiny camera. To give a few examples, they mostly have a precision lens turret or sliding lens panel, and sometimes a built-in electric exposure meter which gives automatically the correct lens stop.

A range of speeds is essential, not forgetting the single-picture device. Reverse drive is not always provided, but its absence is not of consequence.

The lenses are nearly always interchangeable, with apertures up to f 1.5. The lens or lenses are often fitted in a circular or semi-circular turret. The turret may also carry the front element of the finders (p. 26).

The sliding panel carrying two lenses, one of normal focus and the other of long focus, is adopted by German manufacturers, and the pivoted slide by the Americans. The amateur is thus able to use several lenses, and can change rapidly from one to another. The viewfinder field is automatically adjusted to suit the lens in use, immediately indicating the actual field covered by the lens.

Several cameras incorporate a photo-electric type of exposure meter (p. 78). The photo-cell is built into the camera, and is connected to an indicator in the viewfinder field. By simply moving a lever we can make the indicator

The Swiss Paillard Bolex B8 is a turret version of the Bolex C8 (p. 45). The turret (**L3**) carries two lenses, apart from that all features as well as the interior details are the same as for the C8 model. Special points include a cable release socket (**S1**), a shutter speed table for different filming speeds (**S2**), and a wrist strap (**S3**) which screws into the tripod bush (**O4**). For standard features see p. 37.

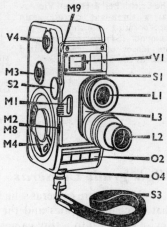

The Swiss Paillard Bolex H8 is an almost professional 8 mm. camera, incorporating practically every possible aid to cinematography. It has a three-lens turret, universal finder, screen focusing finder (**S1**), separate crank shaft for hand drive (**S2**), provision for opening the shutter (**S3**) for gate focusing, a motor clutch (**S4**), a release control (**S5**) for continuous or single frame running, audible footage control (**S6**), as well as a frame counter, special loading aids, and a wide range of accessories. For standard features see p. 37.

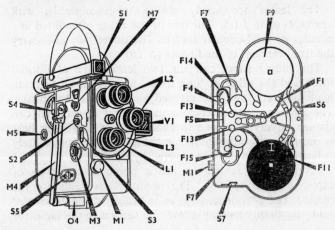

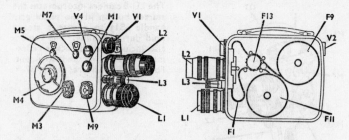

The most advanced model of the French Cine Gel has a two-lens turret (**L3**), a range of speeds, and footage (**M5**) as well as frame (**M7**) counters. For standard features see p. 37.

In the Austrian Eumig C8 the aperture control (**L6**) is coupled to a diaphragm in front of the cell (**S1**) of the built-in photo-electric meter (**S2**). In use the pointer of the meter (visible in the finder) has to be aligned against a fixed mark, by controlling the diaphragm. This automatically sets the lens to the correct aperture. This automatically results in the film getting the correct exposure. It also saves the necessity of removing the camera from the eye for resetting even if lighting conditions change. The film indicator (**S3**) adjusts the meter for different film speeds. A window (**S4**) inside the camera shows the film transport claws. For standard features see p. 37.

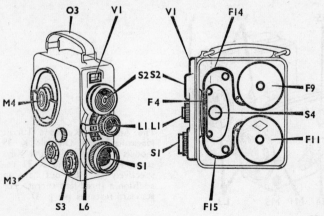

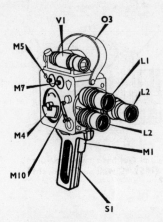

The LD-8 camera incorporates the starter button in the pistol grip handle (SI) to ensure a steady hold during filming. The camera also includes all the other refinements of a high-grade instrument. For standard features see p. 37.

coincide with a fixed mark. This automatically adjusts the aperture for the prevailing light, and can be done while filming, if the light changes.

Such a built-in meter makes taking an almost automatic operation. You can devote your full attention to picture quality, framing composition, and the expression of the subjects, instead of worrying about technical considerations.

The threading of the film has also received close attention.

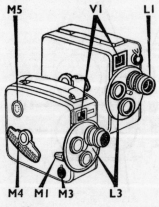

The American Keystone Turret Magazine-8 and Olympic K 35 models are similar to the Keystone Magazine-8 and K 32 respectively (p. 48), but have in addition a three-lens turret. For standard features see p. 37.

The German Nizo Heliomatic camera incorporates a coupled exposure meter and also has interchangeable lenses. The latter are mounted on the same sliding panel as the cell (S1) and all linked together by the knurled ring (S2). The film speeds are set on the dial (S3). An eyepiece at the side (S4) permits the scene to be viewed at right-angles. For standard features see p. 37.

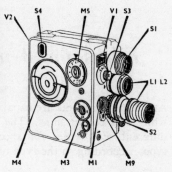

If the camera is not of the charger type, the gate and pressure plate are designed to avoid accidents, which would be out of place in such a camera.

Making the Most of Refinements

The refinements found in cameras of this class are not always superfluous; they make filming more pleasant, and encourage the cameraman to pursue his hobby. Since results are certain, filming with such equipment is always a pleasure.

The exposure meter built into the camera has one minor inconvenience: because of its high sensitivity it is rather fragile. For this reason you must take extra care of the camera.

The use of long-focus lenses for enlarging the subject like a pair of binoculars necessitates a viewfinder of high precision, since a badly framed image is lacking in interest. The subject may move, you have to be able to keep it centred in the viewfinder. So that a precision finder is essential.

59

Films for 8 mm. Cameras

ALL 8 mm. cameras are capable of taking both black-and-white and colour films. The former can be bought with different sensitivities for specific uses, the latter in two types, according to the type of lighting.

Black-and-white Films

Before choosing your film, you should know the different characteristics of the various emulsions obtainable. These details are of importance for your exposure and also when you want to use colour filters to obtain certain effects. The main data you want to know are the colour rendering of the film, its speed or sensitivity and the grain. Let us look at them in turn.

Colour Sensitivity

The film translates all the colours of nature into a scale of half-tones, from black to white.

All 8 mm. films for the amateur are panchromatic, that is to say they are sensitive, and thus react to all visible colours from violet to red. Nevertheless there are certain discrepancies between the brightness of various image tones perceived by the eyes, and the manner in which it is reproduced in black-and-white by the film.

Blue, for example, which our eyes see as a fairly dark colour, is translated as a light grey; that is because films are too sensitive to blue. We can, however, use filters (p. 85) to neutralise this excess sensitivity.

Green, a colour comparatively brilliant in nature, is translated as a medium grey, again contrary to our perception. Equally we can provide correction for this false rendering (p. 86).

Red will come out as light grey or dark grey, according to the type of film we are using, but that is less important in almost every case.

Film Speed

Films are also characterized by their general sensitivity or speed.

Each sensitivity has certain definite uses. Generally it is advisable to employ the slowest film suitable for the job, in order to secure the finest possible grain (p. 62) in the projected image. High sensitivity does not go with fine grain. Very fast films give a grainy image on projection.

The speed or sensitivity of a film is indicated on the carton or on the instruction sheet. It is expressed in degrees BS, Scheiner, DIN, or ASA exposure index numbers. Films of European make have their speed rated in degrees BS, Scheiner or DIN; films manufactured in America have their speed rating indicated in ASA numbers.

In the BS and Scheiner systems, the speed is doubled with every increase of three degrees, so that a film of 26° is twice as fast as one of 23°.

DIN readings are expressed in the form of a fraction, but the speed varies in the same way. Thus films of 23° Scheiner are about equivalent to 13/10° DIN, those of 26° Scheiner to 16/10° DIN.

ASA exposure index numbers always follow an arithmetical progression.

Thus a film of 25 ASA is half as fast as a film of 50, and the latter is half as fast as a film of 100 ASA.

The methods employed to measure films by the various scales are different. But these can be compared approximately (see table, p. 62), so that you can use the approximate equivalent figure if your exposure meter is not scaled by the same units as those in which the film speed is given.

Speed Rating				Types of Emulsions
BS	ASA	Scheiner	DIN	
21°	10	22°	12/10°	Slow colour emulsions.
22°	12	23°	13/10°	
23°	16	24°	14/10°	Very fine-grain emulsions.
24°	20	25°	15/10°	Fast colour emulsions.
25°	25	26°	16/10°	Emulsions of medium speed, for bad
26°	32	27°	17/10°	lighting conditions and artificial light.
27°	40	28°	18/10°	
28°	50	29°	19/10°	
29°	64	30°	20/10°	
30°	80	31°	21/10°	
31°	100	32°	22/10°	Emulsions for very poor lighting
32°	125	33°	23/10°	conditions.

Other Properties of Films

The photographic image is not uniform, but made up of many small spots or grains. If these are comparatively large, the screen image shows a distinctly coarse texture.

A fine-grain emulsion is therefore a necessity for 8 mm. film since the tiny frames are so greatly magnified. Generally speaking, the slower the emulsion the finer the grain.

Films also have a certain exposure latitude. This means that they will still give good results if the exposure is not exactly right. Without this property amateur cinematography would never have attained its present popularity. In practice, with the automatic methods of compensation used in the processing laboratories, variations in exposure of the order of $1\frac{1}{2}$ to 2 lens stops too much or too little can be compensated in development, at least with black-and-white films. As we shall see later (p. 63) colour films have a much smaller latitude, barely half a stop either way.

Types of 8 mm. Film

The amateur can choose from three types of film, according to the type of work he has in mind.

Ultra fine grain film is the ideal film for 8 mm., and the one which the amateur should generally use. Its speed is about 23° to 24° BS or Scheiner—fast enough for most kinds of work. Its extremely fine grain gives a sharp image on the screen, up to 4 or 5 ft. in width, without the grain showing.

Film of medium speed—about 26° or 27° BS or Scheiner, is useful in bad lighting conditions: in bad weather in autumn or winter. On the other hand, it is suitable for use with artificial light only when there is plenty of light. Its fine grain still gives good projected images.

High-speed film of 32° or 33° BS or Scheiner is used only in exceptional circumstances—for shooting in very dull weather, or indoors with comparatively poor light. Its very high speed extends the possibilities of the 8 mm. camera, and enables you to shoot in the worst lighting conditions.

Colour Films

By using colour films you can reproduce on your screen all the beauty and colour that you filmed, without any difficulty, and without special attachments.

The exposure latitude of colour film is very small, and a comparatively small error in the iris setting will upset the colour rendering. The exposure tables generally supplied with the film are not good enough for practical use, and a meter (p. 70) is recommended to ensure correct exposure.

Two types of colour films are made; for daylight and for artificial light, the latter for over-run lamps.

Special compensating filters can be obtained to allow daylight film to be used in artificial light, and conversely for using Type "A" (artificial light) film in daylight. But this method of working cannot be recommended; it is far better to take the film out of the camera and put in another suited to the type of lighting.

The speed of daylight film is 22° to 25° BS or Scheiner. It should be used only in a very good light. It is found in practice that at certain hours of the day—early morning or in the evening—the warm colour of daylight tends to falsify the rendering of colours which become reddish.

Type "A" film for artificial light is specially balanced for use with Photofloods or similar over-run filament lamps. For consistent results it is always advisable to use new lamps with this type of film run at exactly the marked voltage. Other types of lamps such as general service lamps should not be used; in technical language, such light sources have a different colour temperature from Photofloods, which results in the light having a dominant hue for which the film is not balanced.

For these reasons, when shooting with Type "A," use only new Photofloods run at the correct voltage.

Spools

You buy your film in different packings to suit the type of camera. In cameras made to suit special chargers you cannot use spools, and on the other hand in cameras made to suit spools you cannot use chargers. An exception is one type of charger, in which you insert the film on a spool.

With the exception of cameras designed for a charger, all cameras take the normal 25 feet spool of double-eight film.

Double-eight film, as we have already seen, measures 16 mm. in width, and has one perforation for each frame. It is only when you get the processed film back from the processing station that it becomes a single-eight film, ready for projection. So you will have 50 feet of single-eight film instead of 25 feet of double-eight; the original film has been slit in two down the centre, and the two lengths are spliced end to end (p. 10). On some makes of film you can see on the raw stock the dividing line down which the film will be slit after processing and before splicing.

When you buy a double-eight film, 25 feet in length, you

64

get actually a spool containing about 30 or 35 feet. At each end of the usable part, which measures exactly 25 feet, there is a length of leader film.

These leaders are used to thread the film round the sprocket and rollers and through the gate, and to protect the light-sensitive film. They are cut off at the processing station, so do not attempt to film on these leaders.

Double-eight film in 25 feet lengths can be used in any type of camera, even in those built to carry larger spools.

You buy your film in a sealed carton, enclosed in a tin which is hermetically sealed with gummed tape. This packing is suitable for tropical countries. The film itself inside the carton carries a paper band with a guarantee; if this band is torn, you will be wise to refuse the film.

Double-eight film is also supplied on a special 30 feet spool, for use in certain cameras. The film thus runs for 4 minutes on each run, or 8 minutes altogether.

Most cameras use 25-feet spools of double-eight film (*left*). When the first half is exposed the leader often carries the letters "HALF EXP" on it. The single-eight charger (*centre and right*) used in some cameras consists of a metal body (1) which carries the film on a bobbin (4). It goes from there over a guide roller (3), and emerges through a light trap (2). From the camera gate it runs through another light trap and guide roller into the take-up bobbin (5).

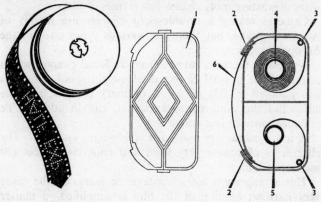

The 100 feet spool is less common, since there are few 8 mm. cameras that will take a spool of this size. The 100 feet spool gives a running time of 16 minutes—8 minutes on each run.

Chargers

There are two types of cameras using chargers: those which take double-eight chargers, and those which take single-eight.

The 25 feet double-eight charger is an American idea, and carries 25 feet of double-eight film. The charger is reversible in the camera—that is to say, at the end of the first run you turn it over exactly as with a spool, so that the side which was formerly the feed roll now becomes the take-up. The film has no leader, because it is protected while loading by the charger.

The use of a charger has a lot of advantages. Loading is extremely simple. Fogging, which so often occurs at the beginning and end of a film when loading in daylight, is avoided where chargers are used.

But perhaps its chief advantage is that you can change from a black-and-white film to a colour film or *vice versa* without wasting more than a few frames of film.

Cameras taking a double-eight charger are mainly of American make, but there are various types also on the European market.

A pre-war German camera used a special charger which contained the normal 25 feet double-eight spool. The film was handled exactly as in an ordinary charger, and the latter has the same advantages, and can in addition be reloaded with 25 feet spools.

A few cameras are made for single-eight chargers. The charger is of course very thin, and contains 33 feet (10 metres) of film.

This arrangement has advantages: cameras can be made very narrow; loading of the film is simplified—a matter

66

The double-eight charger or magazine incorporates its own gate (2), (3), and mechanism. On closing the camera, the button (1) opens the gate aperture. The guide (4) is in contact with the take-up bobbin (6) which is driven through the shaft (7). The film is initially on the feed bobbin (5).

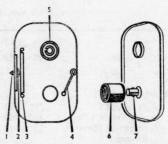

of a couple of seconds, there is no risk of fogging, and films can be changed over without waiting for the end of the roll.

There is yet another advantage over the double-eight charger; the single-eight type contains no internal mechanism, and the risks of jamming and other troubles within the charger are practically nil.

Date of Expiry

On the packing you will find stamped an expiry date. The film should be exposed before that date. When you buy a film, this date should preferably be at least six months ahead, otherwise its use may be limited.

But actually the film is still perfectly usable later than that; the only precaution necessary is to over-expose it very slightly—perhaps half a stop or a stop.

In tropical countries, if the climate is humid, do not rely too much on this expiry date. It is better in such places not to keep your film more than two or three months, otherwise the results of humidity may show on the film. Order your films from home—particularly colour films—as you need them and so avoid unnecessary storage.

In temperate climates the conditions in which the film is stored still affect its keeping properties.

Generally speaking, when you are on a journey, it is better to take with you all the film you will need, rather than buy it here and there.

Film	Speed		Packings	
	BS	ASA	Double-eight	Single-eight

Black-and-white:

Film	BS	ASA	Double-eight	Single-eight
Agfa Isopan F ...	25°	25	25 ft spools	33 ft. chargers.
Ansco Triple S Pan ...	31°	100	25 ft. spools	
Gevapan 23 Micro Reversal	22°	12	25, 50, 100 ft. spools	33 ft. chargers.
Gevaert Gevapan 26 Super Reversal	25°	25	25, 50, 100 ft. spools	33 ft. chargers.
Gevaert Gevapan 32 Ultra Reversal	31°	100	25, 50, 100 ft. spools	33 ft. chargers.
Kodak Super X ...	27°	40	25 ft. spools 25 ft. magazines	
Perutz Perkine U15 ...	25°	25	25 ft. spools	
Perutz Perkine U21 ...	31°	100	25 ft. spools	
Schleussner Adox U17	26°	32	25, 50, 100 ft. spools	

Colour:

Film	BS	ASA	Double-eight	Single-eight
Agfacolor T (Daylight)	25°	25	25 ft. spools	33 ft. chargers.
Anscochrome Daylight	26°	32	25 ft. spools	
Anscochrome Tungsten	26°	32	25 ft. spools	
Kodachrome Daylight	21°	10	25 ft. spools 25 ft. magazines	
Kodachrome Type A	23°	16	25 ft. spools 25 ft. magazines	

Handling the Film

Always load your camera in the shade, even when it is of the charger type, and never in full daylight, otherwise you may fog the film.

In any country your films will be processed free of charge, provided they are returned to the manufacturers.

Don't forget to write your name and address on the label before sending the film for processing. A good idea, when the film is of anything of importance, is to photograph your name and address on the start of the film (naturally on the light-sensitive part). It is quite easy to do this if you have a suitable supplementary lens of 2 or 3 diopters (p. 91).

Double-eight films on spools are sold in sealed cartons. These cartons are practically light-tight, but they are not heat-proof. When sending either exposed or unexposed films abroad, send them by air rather than by boat. In hot countries keep films in some cool place, away from damp

Cameras are light-tight. But don't leave your half-exposed film in the camera for too long. The latent image may fade (especially with colour films) and in any case, a partially unwound film does not keep so well.

When your films come back after processing, don't leave them in their cartons until you have time to edit them. They will keep better in a large tin.

Your films represent irreplaceable memories. Take great care of them, so that in the course of years you will not find them brittle and useless.

The Right Aperture

In cine work the time of exposure is fixed for a given taking speed, and all you have to worry about is to be sure that the lens aperture is correct for the lighting conditions.

Reversal film as used in the cine camera has an appreciable exposure latitude (p. 62)—due partly to the emulsion itself, and largely to the method employed in processing. With black-and-white film errors of as much as a couple of stops up or down will still give reasonably good results, although naturally the correct exposure will give the best results.

With colour film, on the other hand, the aperture must be right; the tolerance is only about half a stop up or down.

Exposure Tables

Most film packings include some sort of simple exposure table which shows the correct aperture for various subjects and lighting conditions. Alternatively, you can use an exposure calculator, such as the *Focal Cine Chart*.

With a calculator you generally select the subject brightness and weather setting, and read off the aperture opposite the speed of the film you are using. With tables you may have to add up appropriate numbers.

In either case you are safe enough with standard conditions and black-and-white film. With colour film, and under difficult lighting conditions it is, however, better to use an exposure meter to measure the light.

Exposure Meters

Exposure meters or photometers are precision instruments, whose job it is to show automatically the correct lens aperture required for any given lighting conditions, taking into account the film stock used and the taking speed.

The commonest exposure meters are photo-electric ones. They are all based upon the same principle: different makes vary only in their appearance and in the method of indicating the lens aperture.

But the fact that these instruments work automatically does not mean that the cameraman does not come into it; the photo-cell, perfect though it may be, cannot think for the cameraman, and cannot interpret the lighting according to his ideas.

How the Meter Works

Every exposure meter has three main components, the cell, the micro-ammeter and the calculator.

The photo-electric cell is simply a metal disc or plate (the anode) and a thin metal coating (the cathode) separated by a semi-conductor. The metal coating is so thin that light passes through it, and produces a minute electric current. This current is read on a highly sensitive galvanometer. The photo-cells used have a high sensitivity; their area is only a fraction of a square inch.

The photo-cell is a delicate piece of apparatus which will eventually wear out, but it can then be easily replaced. The output of the cell may vary from year to year, and the reading of the meter should therefore be checked by some reliable firm.

The micro-ammeter is the most fragile part of the exposure meter. The moving parts have to be extremely light if the instrument is to be sufficiently sensitive. The job of the micro-ammeter is to measure the current generated by the photo-cell when light falls upon it.

Actually the meter does not look like an ordinary electric instrument, it is not graduated in micro-amps., or millionths of an ampere, but its pointer indicates brightness values which must be interpreted by a calculator in order to find the lens aperture required. The scale may be fixed or interchangeable.

In some modern exposure meters it is possible to lock the pointer. This serves two purposes: first to protect the instrument from shocks and vibration; to use the meter, simply press a button which frees the pointer. The second advantage is equally important; after a reading, release the button: the needle remains locked at the reading taken.

Using the Calculator

The object of the calculator is to translate the meter readings into aperture or exposure values. Instruments made specially for cine work read only in stop values, although otherwise they are similar to ordinary photographic types. But actually the majority of instruments are made to suit either cine or photographic work, and this is the most convenient type of instrument to choose.

On the calculator, you will find a scale showing the meter readings, a scale of emulsion speeds, and finally a scale of stop values and sometimes taking speeds.

Meters designed for still cameras carry shutter speed markings. You can just as easily use them for cine work, by reading off the aperture for the exposure time corresponding to the taking speed (below).

The effective exposure time for a given taking speed depends on the shutter opening, which if it differs from the average is generally given in the instruction book. Generally you can reckon that the exposure time at 16 frames is $\frac{1}{30}$ to $\frac{1}{32}$ second, but it may be as short as $\frac{1}{40}$ second.

EXPOSURES AT DIFFERENT SPEEDS

	Taking Speed Frames per Second					
	8	16	24	32	64	72
Corresponding exposure time (seconds)	1/16	1/32	1/48	1/64	1/128	1/144
In round figures	1/15	1/30	1/50	1/60	1/125	1/150

The rounded-off figures are near enough in practice, even for colour.

72

The Field of the Meter

The photo-cell is sensitive to light no matter from what direction it falls; the current is proportional to the total intensity of light. If we want accurate readings, it is necessary to limit the view of the cell so that it covers only the subject area.

The simplest method is by means of a honeycomb which cuts off rays of light reaching the cell obliquely. This honeycomb may be made more efficient by a lens or lenses which concentrate the action of the light while still limiting the oblique rays.

In some meters this idea is replaced by a long flat box, with only a small hole through which the light can reach the cell. Sometimes there is a grating inside this box, which helps still further in keeping out oblique rays.

Whatever means may be used to restrict the field of the cell, it is much less important than one might imagine. When using the brightlight or incident light method of measurement (p. 76) oblique rays have little effect.

Special Meter Features

Some types of exposure meter include an attachment enabling the instrument to be used as an incident light meter—that is to say, measuring the light falling on the subject, and not that reflected by it. The incident light attachment takes the form of a hemisphere, cone or other translucent cover over the photo-cell; this integrates the light reaching the meter from nearly all directions.

Incident light meters are of special value with colour film, as there the overall lighting is the most important factor in exposure determination (p. 79).

So that the markings on the scale should not be too close together at high readings, most meters have some special arrangement for use when the light is very strong. On some meters there is a cap with a small hole, cutting off most of the light; naturally a special scale has to be used when the instrument is fitted with this cap.

Sometimes a resistance is wired in the meter circuit, which reduces the current in bright light. To take readings in a poor light, you simply press a button which short-circuits the resistance. Here again a special scale must be used.

In some modern meters an internal shutter is operated by a knob, cutting off part of the light.

Photometers

Photometers measure the light in a different way. By means of a small telescope you can examine a tiny portion of the scene—for instance the cheek or forehead of your sitter, or a back-light in the hair—and compare its brightness with a standard light source built into the meter. In that way you can adjust your exposure to that particular spot. If you are filming an exceptionally contrasty scene such separate readings are much more helpful than general ones and should always be taken.

Reflected Light Readings

The majority of exposure meters measure the light reflected from the subject. The results obtained are reasonably satisfactory, but sometimes need corrections. This is how you go about determining the exposure.

First set your meter to the correct speed of the film you are using, and the speed at which you are shooting. Hold

For reflected light readings approach the subject until it completely fills the field of view of the exposure meter. Otherwise a very bright or very dark background may influence the meter and lead to incorrect readings.

the meter as close as possible to the subject, pointing towards it. Note the meter reading, which represents the amount of light reflected by the subject.

Although the meter cannot make allowances for all the different conditions met with, the exposure latitude of reversal film generally ensures good results. But remember the following points:

The exposure meter is affected not only by the light reflected by the subject, but equally by its surroundings and background. The same subject placed in front of a light background and a dark background *should* give the same reading, but in practice the background affects the meter reading. Unless you hold your meter close to the subject, the picture on the screen will not be at all what you had expected.

A dark background means that your meter indicates a larger stop. If the meter readings are followed without corrections, the background will be correctly reproduced, but your subject will be over-exposed, lacking in detail and modelling.

A light background on the other hand means that your meter will indicate a smaller stop. Unless you correct the reading, your subject will be dark and not at all like the original.

So get as close as possible to your subject, in order to pick up as little as possible of the light from the surroundings.

When the meter is placed near your subject—say a person—the reading will need yet another correction. In a cine picture the features are generally the most important part, and consequently the aperture must be set for correct exposure of the face. If you overlook this point your meter will give different readings according to whether the person is wearing dark or light clothes. In either case, the features may be wrongly exposed.

When you take a reading of an open view and point the meter towards the horizon, it is affected by various sources of reflected light—the ground near by, by water, if there is any, and by the sky. If the meter is moved about it will give different readings according to where you point it.

In this case, to keep the exposure within the latitude of your emulsion, and to give the most correct rendering of distant details, close down one or two stops below what seems to be the most accurate meter reading. On the other hand, if there is any water in the foreground, do just the reverse—open up the iris one stop or so, otherwise the distant scenery will be rendered too dark.

With normal landscapes the sky is generally the brightest part of the scene; though it is not always the most important part, it has the greatest effect on the meter. If you normally base your readings on a close-up view, point the meter downwards so as to exclude the sky.

Indoors

When filming people by artificial light switch on only those light sources which provide the principal lighting on the face. Side and back lighting will improve the final shot, but should have little or no effect upon the exposure required. Such light sources may, however, shine into the cell of the exposure meter and thus produce too high a reading. If, of course, side lighting is unusually strong, it may be necessary to work at one stop down, especially if it is to play a major part in your lighting scheme.

Incident Light Readings

This term simply means that you measure the light falling on the subject, instead of the light reflected from it. It is more interesting, and for the amateur possibly simpler, to fix your exposure by measuring the incident light.

Hold your exposure meter, with its opal cap or cone clipped on so that the cap receives the same light as is falling on the subject. Hold the meter near the subject, but *pointing towards the camera.*

76

When you cannot get near enough to the subject, it is good enough to hold the meter, still pointing towards the camera, in such a way that the cap over the cell receives the same light as the subject.

The basis of our measurements is the intensity of light falling upon the subject. Whether the subject is light or dark—whether it is near or far off—it is still the same sunshine that throws light within the same angle. We no longer have to worry about the colour of the subject or its reflecting power. The meter is scaled in such a manner that your film records a range of tones corresponding to those of the subject when you set the lens aperture according to the meter reading. When you think of it, this way of using the meter should guarantee good results with most subjects.

Outdoors, objects near the camera or the background behind the subject will no longer have the same effect as when you work by the reflected light method. It is only the incident light that determines what stop you work at.

For open views it is just as easy to work this way, except in a few difficult cases. Just stand in front of the camera, hold your meter—with its opal cap on—pointing towards the lens. Always take the precaution to see that the meter receives the same light as your distant subject. If the subject is in shadow, while there is no shade close at hand (a state of affairs often found, for instance on race tracks or sports grounds) you can imitate the correct conditions by holding something over the meter to cast a shadow.

Indoors your subject is always accessible. Just switch on all the lighting you are going to use, including modelling lamps, and take your reading.

The Key Tone Method

Yet another way of using a reflected light meter is to measure the light reflected from a standard grey key tone. When the light is directly in front of the subject or only slightly to the side, this gives the same accuracy of results as an incident light meter. The principle is again that if you tie down the exposure to a particular lighting level—which is what the light reflected from the grey tone measures—all the tones of the subject will reproduce in their right brightness on the film.

The grey tone should ideally reflect about 18-20 per cent. of the light it receives. This figure of 18 per cent. has not been chosen arbitrarily; it is the average proportion of light reflected by a normal subject—neither bright nor dark. The value corresponds therefore to what will look right in projection, provided the camera aperture is set accordingly.

You can easily produce such a standard key tone by exposing a piece of photographic paper and developing it. Use a contrasty matt bromide paper, and so that you can more easily control the density during development, add some anti-foggant. Expose it so that it will develop slowly in three or four minutes.

The tone required looks a medium grey. It is best to expose and develop several sheets of paper and measure them with an exposure meter to see which is nearest to the required tone.

That is not as complicated as it sounds, for we can assume that white paper, such as the base of bromide paper, reflects about 90 per cent. of the light falling on it. To check your grey tone, therefore, take a sheet of this white paper (e.g. an unexposed but fixed out sheet of bromide paper)

For the key tone method of taking readings, point the meter at a grey card held in such a way as to receive the same light as the subject.

and take a close-up reading of it in good light with a reflected light type of exposure meter. Take care not to cast a shadow on the paper with your meter, but bring it close enough so that the paper fills the field of view of the photo-cell.

Then take a similar reading of each of your grey test pieces. For the correct grey, the meter should indicate one-fifth of the white paper reading. If the meter is scaled in apertures, this corresponds to just over two stops larger—e.g., f 2 instead of f 4.5, or f 2.8 instead of f 6.3 or f 3.5 instead of f 8.

For convenience in use, mount your grey sheet on a piece of card.

To use the key tone, hold the card in front of the subject, facing the camera.

Take a reading by holding the meter in front of the grey chart, and as close as possible to it. Take care that no stray light falls upon the cell, and that your shadow does not fall on the card.

Generally speaking, all types of reflected-light meters can be used in this way. But before relying on the method, check your first results, and if any adjustments are necessary, make them in future.

Controlling Contrast

When your subject includes a wide range of tones—very bright and very dark surfaces—the incident light meter or the key tone method will still give the proper readings for each of these tones. But your emulsion cannot reproduce correctly the whole range of tones which we often find in nature; often you can reduce the extremes of contrast by using additional lighting or a reflector.

Colour film especially cannot reproduce faithfully any subject with strong contrasts. The ratio between the brightest object and the darkest should not exceed 3 to 1. Therefore check the brightness range by close-up reading with a reflected light meter or with a photometer, pointing it at the lightest and darkest parts of the scene. If the contrast is greater than the permissible 3 : 1 ratio use additional lighting or reflectors, so as to keep within the limits of your film.

Built-in Exposure Meters

With some cameras a photo-cell and its micro-ammeter are built into the camera. The amount of light falling on the cell is controlled by means of an iris which is opened or closed to suit the light, and the knob which adjusts this iris also sets the lens iris. The pointer is seen in the camera view-finder.

To take a reading, you simply adjust the irises until the pointer is opposite a fixed mark, when you can be sure that the setting is correct. Naturally you must first set the meter for the speed of the emulsion and the taking speed.

With black-and-white films this system gives perfectly satisfactory results. With colour films the readings are generally near enough.

When panning the camera (p. 108) or taking any scene needing constant adjustment of exposure (for example, children playing in sunshine and shadow) such a built-in type of meter is very valuable. The stop can be altered

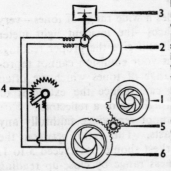

In a coupled exposure meter the meter elements are a photo-electric cell with an iris diaphragm (6), a micro-ammeter (2), and a variable resistance (4) which is set according to the speed of the film in the camera. In use, the diaphragm (6) in front of the photo-cell is opened or closed until the pointer—usually visible in the finder window (3)—is central. As the diaphragm (6) is coupled to the lens aperture (1) via the gear wheel (5), setting the meter automatically stops down the lens to the right aperture.

moment by moment while taking. The pointer will react to the least change in light; you simply have to adjust the iris to keep the point on its mark.

In a long panning shot, where a number of different exposures are required, the stops will be correct from beginning to end.

On the other hand, the built-in exposure meter makes your camera rather more fragile. It must be handled with still greater care, since the more sensitive a meter, the more fragile it is.

A built-in meter does tend to limit the use of different lenses. You must be satisfied with the lens or lenses fitted to your camera, although you can use an afocal system to alter the focus.

The Meter in Practice

Working out the exposure should not be a long or complicated procedure. Ideally we ought to be able to translate the reading directly into the lens stop required. To do this we first have to eliminate the main variables.

The easiest way of doing that is to allow for all of them by the film speed setting. This will depend partly on the rated speed of the film, and partly on the way in which you use the meter.

Make a few tests, therefore, measuring the light by whatever method you propose to use—reflected light (p. 74), incident light (p. 76) or key tone (p. 77). Run off about 2 feet of film for each test, using a different film speed setting on the meter every time. Repeat this for different types of subjects, then project your test film to see which film speed setting gives the best exposed result.

The maker's speed figure can usually be taken as a basis for the test, but the ideal figure may still need modification for various factors. Those you will learn by experience.

For instance, if you have a low-power projector you will have to make allowance on your meter readings to obtain

When taking exposure meter readings of average subjects (*left*) use the reflected or incident light method without correction. Inaccessible subjects (*right*) permit a normal reflected light reading, but for an incident light reading point the meter towards the sun and use one stop smaller to compensate for the increase in light.

a thin image. In other words you must use a lower film speed figure on the calculator.

Or, your meter may be old, and not registering so efficiently as a new instrument.

Also, because of the lack of standardisation in the calibration meters do vary in their readings. A comparison of the readings of two meters of different makes on the same scene will convince you of this.

With subjects of high contrast (*left*) take separate reflected light readings of high-light and shadow, and use a mean value. For incident light readings point the cell at the camera. For silhouette effects (*right*) use normal reflected light readings.

With seascapes and similar subjects (*left*) use one stop larger than the reflected or incident light reading indicates. When taking incident readings point the meter at the sky. If the subject has a very brilliant background (*right*) use one stop smaller than the value obtained by incident or reflected light readings.

Taking Care of the Meter

A photo-electric cell will deteriorate in time, even though it is not often used. The needle of the meter may stick or move slowly, or very often will not go to the end of the scale, even in a bright light.

Generally speaking you can reckon that the cell has a life of three years. At the end of this time, you should return

For strongly back-lit subjects (*left*) take a reflected light reading on the figure and use one stop smaller. With incident light readings use the stop obtained. With contrasty against-the-light shots (*right*) use one stop larger than recommended by a reflected light reading, or one stop smaller than given by the incident light reading.

your meter to the maker for a check-up. Do not send it to a repair shop fitted with any old equipment, but failing the maker, to a properly equipped laboratory.

You can always make a rough check on the meter when you project your films. If the pictures are consistently too thin—showing that they are over-exposed—the needle has become sticky and is not registering accurately.

A new meter may make you use too small a stop. There are two answers: either you can temporarily increase the power of your projection lamp, or if the readings continue to be wrong, you can work to a slightly larger stop. Check your meter each season.

With the exception of those meters in which the pointer can be locked, all exposure meters are very delicate instruments. Treat them as such—remember the meter has to read currents of millionths of an ampere. Protect your meter against shake or prolonged vibration. Carry it either in the camera case or in your jacket or waistcoat pocket—not in a trousers pocket. In a car, do not place the meter on the floor or on the ledge under the dash. Either carry it in your pocket, or if it is in the camera case put this on the seat, and not on the floor. On a cycle, carry the meter always in your waistcoat pocket.

Do not expose the cell to light except when using it.

The moving parts of a meter are difficult to repair, and if you have an accident it is generally better to have the whole mechanism changed, rather than try to repair it.

The zero setting of the pointer can be adjusted by means of a screw either at the back of the instrument, or below it. If the pointer cannot be set to zero, have the meter checked.

When you are filming, hang the meter on a cord round your neck; don't let it swing on the end of the cord, but put it in your pocket as soon as you have taken the reading.

To repeat, your exposure meter is an instrument of precision and fragility; treat it with care if you want it to give satisfaction. If you should drop it, return it to the manufacturers for checking.

Using Filters

COLOUR filters are useful in amateur filming:

To correct the colour rendering of black-and-white films;

To create special effects;

To soften the hardness of summer sunshine;

For colour films, special colour filters are available for certain occasions (p. 88).

Filter Mounts

For every type of camera a range of colour filters is available, made of coloured glass. They are set in permanent mounts, and screw or clip on to the lens mount. This type of mount is very simple, but a little impracticable and not economical. To make full use of your camera, it is better to use a universal mount, with a lens-hood.

The front part of a universal mount pulls or screws off so that an unmounted coloured glass or supplementary lens can be used, screwing in the same way into the mount, which in its turn screws or clips on to the lens mount. This arrangement is exceedingly practical; you can change your filters and use numerous types, even though they are not provided by the camera makers.

In one Continental lens, filters are incorporated in the lens itself, and are brought into position by movement of a ring.

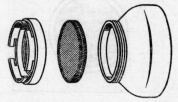

A combined filter holder and lens hood consists of a mount to fit on to the camera lens, the filter glass, and the lens hood which screws into the mount and keeps the glass in position.

Normally the front glass of the lens is sufficiently shielded by the mount, and a lens hood is placed in front of the camera lens; then a lens hood is absolutely essential, since the filter or supplementary lens is exposed to stray light.

Colour Filters for Black-and-white Films

Yellow Filters. A medium yellow is the most useful of filters. Normally it is used to correct the excessively light rendering of blues, and the aperture must then be opened up by one stop (a doubling of the exposure). The yellow filter is useful, too, for country scenes, to show up clouds in a bright sky, which without a filter records as just an expanse of white. In particular, the yellow filter improves the rendering of blond hair.

Orange Filters. These can be used for the same purposes as a yellow filter, but give more contrast. Exposure should be increased by $1\frac{1}{2}$ or 2 stops (3 or 4 times).

In summer an orange filter is useful at the seaside, when your exposure meter indicates a very small aperture, and the lens cannot close down smaller than f 11 or f 16. In this case, when using an orange filter the exposure must be as accurate as possible, otherwise contrasts will be exag-

A yellow filter (*left*) is useful for average landscapes, close-ups of fair-headed people against blue sky, and light cloud effects. Use one stop larger. A yellow green filter (*right*) is mainly intended for masses of foliage and possibly to reduce excessive subject contrast. Open up the aperture by one stop.

The orange filter (*left*) yields stronger contrasts than the yellow, and is suitable for mountain scenery, water, and long distance shots in general. With normal pan film open the lens aperture by two stops. The red filter (*right*) should be used for special effects only, such as night shots in daylight. It exaggerates contrast, rendering blue, violet, and green tones nearly black. With normal pan film use three to four stops larger.

gerated. It is best to try first a yellow filter, and reserve the orange for night effects, and for filming stormy skies. There you have to underexpose otherwise you will not get the desired effect.

Red Filters. Normally a red filter should be used only for distant scenery in fine weather, for instance with a long-focus lens. The filter factor is about 6 or 8 times, or $2\frac{1}{2}$ to 3 stops. The red filter is most often used to produce night effects, by shooting with a clear sky and under-exposing. On the screen, the adequately lit parts of the scene will look as though they had been taken at night and the rest of the image will be without detail.

Ultra-violet Filters. In high mountains ultra-violet radiations are very strong, and the effect is to veil distant scenery. To eliminate this effect, or at least reduce it, ultra-violet absorbing filters are used. They appear colourless, or very slightly tinted. The ultra-violet filter does not need any alteration of the aperture. It is particularly useful above 4,000 or 5,000 feet. Be careful to distinguish between colourless ultra-violet absorbing filters, and ultra-violet selecting filters, which range in colour from deep purple to black.

87

Other Filters. Yellow-green and grey filters tend to reduce the contrast of the image, and are rarely used in cine work.

Grey or neutral filters serve to reduce light intensity in summer, when the lens cannot be stopped down far enough to suit the reading of the exposure meter, which may show f 22 or f 32. The neutral filter has no effect upon colours, but it absorbs part of the light before it reaches the lens, so that it is possible to set the lens at an aperture at which there is no over-exposure. In practice, a yellow or orange filter serves the same purpose, and often gives a better colour rendering.

Neutral filters are obtainable in a range of densities.

Filters for Colour Films

With colour films you need special filters which serve one of two purposes:

1. To neutralize haze or dominant blue casts.
2. To suit the colour balance of the film to the light source, where required.

Haze filters are very pale yellow and usually are available in three intensities.

The pale haze filters reduce the excessive blueness of water and snow scenes, distant views and mountains. They correspond to the ultra-violet filter (p. 87), and the latter can be used for the purpose.

The medium haze filter acts in the same way, but the effect is more pronounced. It counteracts the coolness of the light on a dull day.

The deeper haze filters are required mainly for subjects in the shade, lit by the light of the blue sky.

Conversion filters are also available when you have to use artificial light type film in daylight, and *vice versa*, but they should be employed in emergencies only. Use the conversion filter recommended by the manufacturer of the film.

For specially accurate work you can get a series of colour compensation filters which will serve to standardise the colour of the light. Such filters may be essential for the professional, but the amateur hardly needs them.

You can get filters made of gelatine, which must be mounted between two optical flats, and which are very useful for either the amateur or professional photographer, but they are still not of much value to the cine worker. The trouble is that the additional glass and filter surfaces, although they may correct the colour rendering, also affect the sharpness of the image, especially in 8 mm. For this reason, use filters of mass-dyed glass in preference to gelatine filters, whenever possible.

FILTERS FOR COLOUR FILM

Filter	Purpose	Colour	Increase Aperture by
Light Haze:			
Ansco U.V.15 Ilford Q Wratten No. 1 Wratten No. 2B Lifacolour I	Cuts ultra-violet rays	Colourless or very pale yellow	No increase needed
Medium Haze:			
Ansco U.V.16 Wratten No. 81 Lifacolour II	For distant views, dull days	Pale yellow	½ Stop
Deeper Haze:			
Ansco U.V.17 Ilford No. 102 Wratten No. 81B Lifacolour III	For subjects lit by blue sky	Yellow	1 Stop
Colour Conversion:			
Wratten No. 85	For Kodachrome Type "A" used in daylight	Salmon	½ Stop
Ansco No. 11	For Anscochrome Tungsten used in daylight	Pale Yellow	½ Stop

Polarising Screens

The polarising screen is a special kind of filter. It has the peculiarity of passing only light waves which are polarised—i.e., vibrate in a single direction. Light that has been polarised, either artificially by a polarising screen or by nature, can then be controlled by another polarising screen. By turning the second screen in relation to the first you can reduce or completely cut out the light passed by the camera lens.

When you look obliquely at the surface of the water in a pond, the reflections of the light prevent you seeing to the bottom of the pond. But the rays which reach your eyes have been polarised by reflection from the surface of the water. Consequently it is possible to neutralise this reflected light by means of a polarising screen. Simply look at the subject through the screen and turn it until the reflections disappear.

In practice, to ensure correct adjustment of the screen—for the slightest error in setting it changes the effect—a double polarising screen should be used. There two screens are connected by gearing so that they turn together; one is fitted in front of the lens, and the other away from the optical axis. Look through the second screen and turn it until you get the desired effect; this automatically adjusts the taking screen.

If two polarising screens are mounted on the optical axis, one in front of the other before the lens, and one of them is arranged to turn in relation to the other, we have a fade-out device. When the planes of polarisation are parallel the image is visible, but when one of the screens is gradually turned through 90° the light dims down to complete extinction.

Useful Accessories

Supplementary Lenses

SUPPLEMENTARY lenses, or portrait attachments, should always form part of the cine amateur's kit. They make it possible for the camera lens to focus at shorter distances than the lens mount permits.

With a focusing type of lens, it is possible to focus down to about 18 inches. But by fitting a supplementary lens you can focus down to 12, 9, 6 or even 4 inches. All you need is a supplementary lens of the right type.

The supplementary lens is a converging lens, and is made in different focal lengths. These lenses are not always marked in focal lengths, but in diopters; this marking shows just where to place your subject.

If we want to film a subject say 10 inches distant, then theoretically (and theory is what counts here) we must use a supplementary lens of 10 inches focal length, or 4 diopters. The diopter is a metric term; to work out the number of diopters of a lens, divide 100 by the focal length in centimetres (1 in. is roughly 2.5 centimetres). So that 10 inches =25 cm.; and $100 \div 25 = 4$ diopters.

In the same way, a lens intended to work at a distance of 1 foot (=about 30 cm.) will have a power of $100 \div 30$, or about 3 diopters. Conversely, a lens of 5 diopters will enable you to work at a distance of $100 \div 5 = 20$ cm. or 8 inches.

Working with Supplementary Lenses

Always set the camera lens to infinity, then place your subject at exactly the distance indicated by the power of the supplementary lens used. For example, to film a title card with a lens of 4 diopters, or 10 inches focal length, first set the camera lens to infinity, then clip the 4-diopter supplementary lens on the camera lens, and shield it with a lens hood. Place the card exactly 10 inches from the supplementary lens.

When using a supplementary lens, always measure the distance from the supplementary lens, and not from the camera lens. When you are not using a supplementary lens you can, practically speaking, measure from the front of the camera case.

Makers of inexpensive cameras fitted with fixed-focus lenses are rarely generous with the technical information they give—possibly in case they should misrepresent their products. With fixed-focus cameras, always use a supplementary lens made by the actual camera maker, which will be corrected for the exact focal settings of the camera lens.

Actually such a lens is focused not on infinity, but at an average distance which is rarely given in the instruction books. This distance is so computed that at an average aperture the depth of field will cover the subjects from infinity down to 6 or 8 feet.

With a focusing lens camera, it does not matter whether the supplementary lens is made by the camera maker; any good optician will sell you lenses of the power you need in diopters.

Supplementary lenses of this type should preferably be used in the same screw type mount previously described for filters (p. 85). A colour filter can be used in addition to a supplementary lens, but this will mean double mounting, because the curved face of the lens will prevent the two glasses going together into the single mount. In such a case, it is better to put the supplementary lens nearer the camera lens, with a lens hood to shield both lens and filter.

Some filter mounts have slits through which light may pass. With these mounts, always place the slit in such a position that light does not fall upon it, otherwise you may get flare spots from the light falling through the slit.

Tripods

The most important point about filming is to keep the camera steady. A tripod is therefore almost essential. While a cine tripod makes an excellent photographic stand, the reverse is not the case. Choose your tripod very carefully, and be sure that it is of the right type for cine work. The camera is not a heavy inert mass; the motor may give rise to vibration, and an ordinary photographic tripod is not rigid enough to ensure a picture any steadier than when the camera is hand-held.

The legs must be reasonably strong, with at most three sections. These sections telescope, and they must be locked by tightening screws, and not by spring catches. Tightening screws have other advantages—the tripod is steadier because the legs are securely locked, and the camera can be easily levelled without the use of a ball-and-socket fitting.

The tripod must be high enough, having regard to the height of the cameraman, and taking account of the height of the tripod head and of the camera itself. The legs must be long enough, too, to be well splayed for maximum stability.

Your tripod should have a carrying case. Like all metal equipment, both the legs and the head must be occasionally oiled or greased, otherwise the head will become stiff in action, and your camera will move in jerks.

A telescopic extension can be fitted to a cine tripod making it easier to raise and lower the camera.

Tripod Heads

The tripod head permits the camera to be turned or tilted without moving the tripod itself.

The cine type of tripod head is quite different from an ordinary photographic head. In most types the camera can move in two directions only, vertically and horizontally. Two clamps serve to lock the camera in any position.

The method of securing the camera must be carefully

examined. Avoid tripod heads of aluminium or similar alloys. Check carefully the camera fixing screw, particularly if your camera is a heavy one; this is a detail which the manufacturer is apt to overlook—but it is a matter about which you must be very particular; the life of your camera may depend on it.

The head is moved in any direction by means of a "joystick" or an arm sticking out behind the camera. In addition a couple of rods may be fitted below the front of the camera, for the purpose of carrying various attachments, such as sunshades, masks, shutters, and trick accessories. All these items you can buy separately as and when you need them.

Other Supports

The amateur will not always need a tripod when working with lenses of normal focus. One soon learns to hold the camera steady. A camera grip carrying the release knob is helpful.

With a long-focus lens camera shake is far more noticeable than with a normal lens. A tripod is necessary, otherwise the picture will be jumpy on the screen. If you have no tripod, it is better to shoot at 24 frames a second when camera shake will be less noticeable.

For moving shots with a normal lens, a tripod improves the steadiness and sharpness of the picture, but there is a risk that it may make it more difficult to follow the movement.

The neck sling, which consists of a telescopic rod supported by a strap passing round the neck, can often be used instead of a tripod, even with long-focus lenses. It is quite easy to make such a fitting; the most important part is the telescopic rod. For this, material of a section which may be useful for other purposes can be used; the slide and telescopic parts are secured by locking rings. The system of fixed notches, as is found on some photographic tripods, is not suitable, because the height cannot be easily adjusted, whereas with a telescopic support fitted with locking rings the tubes can be locked in any position.

Viewing Screen

The eye accommodates itself to contrasts more easily than the film can record them. The film tends to exaggerate lighting differences, while the eye sees them as perfectly natural.

A piece of coloured glass held in front of your eyes serves as a viewing screen, and shows what the scene really looks like to the film. The coloured glass largely neutralises colour contrasts and tends to exaggerate subject contrasts. It shows when you may need additional lighting to avoid a too contrasty picture in projection.

Faceted Lens Attachments

These produce two, three or more images of the subject according to the number of prismatic faces. Faceted lenses are mounted in front of the camera lens, and can be either kept stationary during a shot, or turned, when the pictures formed by the prismatic faces will rotate around a central point.

Do not use these attachments for scenery or distant objects, but only on close-ups. The image is multiplied as many times as there are facets on the lens. If your camera will run backwards an exact number of frames, each facet can be successively uncovered, and a different scene filmed with each; the film being run backwards after every exposure.

A faceted lens will need increased exposure, depending on the quality of the workmanship and the material used. Generally it will be not less than $1\frac{1}{2}$ stops. However, the maker will give all necessary instructions concerning exposure.

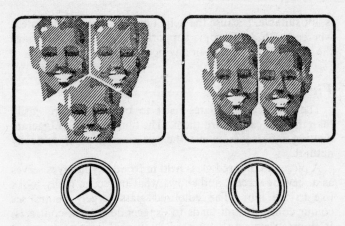

Prismatic lenses can reproduce a subject as many times in the image area as there are facets. They may be in a fixed or rotating mount.

Rangefinders

For distances beyond 6 or 8 feet the depth of field of the lens makes exact measurement of the distance unnecessary. But when we have to work quite close to the camera for large close-ups this no longer applies.

The lens mount can generally be focused down to 18 inches. Between 18 inches and 6 feet a rangefinder can be used, which can be fixed to the top of the camera.

All rangefinders work on the same principle. Two images have to coincide, one being stationary, while the other moves as the knob is turned. When the two images coincide or superimpose, the distance is read on the dial, or on an internal scale.

In one type of rangefinder an internal scale gives distances from infinity down to 18 inches, and a second scale from 18 to 12 inches. When no supplementary lens is used these distances should be measured from the front face of the camera, but when a supplementary lens is fitted to the camera lens, distance must be measured from this lens.

Shooting A Film

WE have now examined the camera and its operations, and the materials, so let us get down to the actual technique of filming.

Choosing your Film Stock

Most of your shots are likely to be exteriors. Whenever possible use an ultra-fine-grain stock with a speed of about 22° or 23° Scheiner (p. 61). This type of film is suitable for most subjects. Never use a faster film when this fine-grain film will serve.

For interior shots with artificial lighting, it is better to use a rather faster film; a speed of 26° or 27° Scheiner is very suitable. It will also serve for outdoor shots in bad weather, in early morning, or late in the evening, or when you want to use a deep filter (orange or red) to obtain trick effects. You will generally need this film during the winter.

Shoot on a film of 32° Scheiner or 100 ASA for interior shots by daylight, when it is impossible to use artificial lighting. Unfortunately this high speed does not go with a fine grain, and you will find your pictures will show less detail and definition than with slower film stocks.

Actually the graininess is not too troublesome, and there are occasions when you have to sacrifice some degree of image quality in order to get a picture at all. With these fast stocks you can work even in quite bad lighting conditions.

Naturally when circumstances are unfavourable you must bear in mind other possibilities, such as the use of a large lens stop, or a running speed of 8 or 12 frames.

Some film stocks give you a warm-tone image which is

very pleasing, and quite different from the usual blue-black tones. These films give the best modelling and an extended range of half-tones.

When you expose a film by artificial light, the speed number on the packing or in the instruction leaflet does not apply. You must set your exposure meter to a different speed, generally lower than the daylight figure. A film shown as 100 ASA or 32° Scheiner in daylight would have a speed of only about 64 ASA or 30° Scheiner to artificial light.

Before accepting a roll of film, check the date on it. Even if the date on a film has expired the film is still quite usable, provided it has been properly stored, but all the same, when you buy a film make sure that the date is as far ahead as possible (p. 67).

In hot countries use fresh films straight from home and buy them as and when you need them. Tropical packing is quite effective against humidity, but not against heat, and the turns of film may possibly stick together due to long storage at high temperatures.

Loading your Camera

Even with a charger type of camera, always load and unload your camera in the shade—some place away from light and dust. If you load or unload in broad daylight or sunlight you risk fogging a considerable length of film.

When you are loading a spool of film first remove the take-up spool which is always inside the camera.

Open the gate. Clean the inside of your camera thoroughly with a small brush, or better with a puff of air from one of those rubber balls used in hair sprayers.

After every roll clean out the gate aperture. It is not always easy to get at this part of the camera, but it is nevertheless important to keep it absolutely free from dirt. Otherwise you will see a jagged frame-line on every frame of your film—and on every subsequent roll of film so long as dirt remains in the aperture.

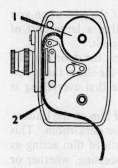
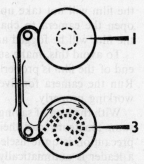

When loading a camera with double-eight spools, first thread the film (2) from the feed spool (1) through the film gate. Then fasten it on the take-up spool (3), and run the camera for a second to make sure the transport works properly. The emulsion side must always face the lens.

Place the spool of film upon the feed spindle, and unwind gently 8 or 10 inches of film. Thread the film first round the sprocket if there is one, next in the gate, taking care to form a loop as is generally indicated inside the camera. The loops may be larger, but never smaller; take care they do not touch any part of the camera.

Before going any further, close the gate and make sure that the film is properly threaded in the gate.

Form the second loop, and if the camera has a sprocket, thread the film underneath it.

Press the starting button and run a few inches of film by the motor, to check the threading.

In some cameras there is a safety device which prevents the camera running until the door is closed; but it is possible to make a check by pressing a release knob (usually the instruction book will indicate this).

If the film runs correctly, carry on with the threading. Insert the end of the film into the narrow slit in the take-up spool.

Many hold-ups are caused by this last operation. The end of the film may accidentally slip out of the slot, when the film will not take up. At the end of the reel when you open the camera to change over the film, a large part of the film will be fogged and hopelessly spoilt.

To avoid this, make sure before closing the door that the end of the film is properly inserted into the slit in the spool. Run the camera for five seconds to see that everything is working properly.

With the idea of saving a few inches of film on the leaders, some amateurs load their cameras in the dark-room. This precaution is quite useless, for the length of film acting as a leader is automatically cut off in processing, whether or not it has been exposed.

Inserting a Charger

The insertion of a charger is less complicated than loading with a spool.

Open the door, slip the charger into the space provided for it, making sure that the film goes into the gate. Close the door, which automatically releases the pressure pad to flatten the film against the aperture in the gate.

In a charger of American make, the film is totally enclosed, and two shutters protect the taking apertures.

Setting the Footage Counter

In many cameras the counter automatically goes back to the starting point—which is before the point marked "0"—when the door is opened. Run through the leader until the figure "0" appears opposite the mark, when the usable part of the film will be in the gate.

Other types of counters have to be re-set by hand. Turn the counter right backwards, and run the motor until the figure "0" appears, which indicates the actual start of the film.

Some counters make use of the "feeler" system, which is more or less accurate according to how tightly the film is wound. To find the start of the film, count for 12 to 15

Hold the camera absolutely steady while taking. Lean against a tree or a wall wherever practicable to gain the support for a firm hold.

seconds, and then note the position of the moving scale in relation to the mark.

Some counters "count backwards" instead of adding (like the scoring in darts). The beginning of the film is shown as "25", which means that 25 feet of film are waiting to be exposed.

Taking a Scene

We are now ready for an actual shot.

First check the camera controls (focus, aperture, camera speed) and wind the motor.

Mount the camera on a tripod (p. 93) where practicable,

Make use of any available opportunities for additional support, when crouching, lying or sitting down and try to rest your elbows.

and view the scene through the finder to check the framing.

Finally, press the starter button and keep it pressed down for the required time.

If you are taking a hand-held shot, hold the camera as steady as possible. Lean against a suitable support for extra firmness. Any camera movements (p. 107) must be absolutely smooth.

Remember to rewind the motor after each take. Also check the footage counter every time to make sure you have enough film left for the proposed shot. Nothing is more annoying than a break in the middle of a take because the film has run out.

At the end of the film put the cap on the lens, and run the motor until the trailer has gone through. Then, with double-eight film change over the spools to run off the second half, or unload.

In one double-eight charger the film has no leaders, and the second part can be run immediately by reversing the charger.

A single-eight charger holds only 33 feet of film. When this has been run through, you simply replace the charger by a new one, and resume shooting.

Unloading

Just as when loading, always unload the camera in the shade, away from light and dust. If the film has only been exposed down one side, change over the spools and run the second half. At this stage, the spool which you bought with the film is placed on the take-up spindle. As before, make very certain that the end of the film is securely fixed in the slot. The slot may be wider than that of the spool supplied with the camera; the majority of accidents which cost a considerable footage of film arise from lack of this precaution.

The usable part of the film measures exactly 25 feet and gives you rather more than four minutes of shooting time, at normal speed. This length is the same with all makes of film.

The length of the leaders before and after the usable length of film varies with different manufacturers; generally speaking you can reckon on an average length of 4 feet or more at each end.

Colour films have rather longer leads.

Length of Scenes

A film consists of a series or sequence of scenes relating to one general subject.

Keep your scenes short! The beginner tends to make his scenes too long, and consequently to waste film. Sooner or later he will cut these too long scenes.

It is hardly possible to make any hard and fast rules for the length of scenes. Every rule has its exceptions: all one can say is that it is the subject that must fix the length of scene.

However, as a practical rule it is best to keep to an average length of 8 to 10 seconds for each scene or each camera angle—for the scene may be filmed from different angles or at different distances. But while the camera is focused on one subject, don't run for more than 8 or 10 seconds. If the scene is longer it becomes tedious—if it is shorter your audiences will not have time to take it in.

To time your shots an audible footage counter is very useful, but not every camera has it.

If you count 10 seconds starting from 1, you will not be right or anywhere near right. Experience shows that while taking it is difficult, if not impossible, to mark the end of every second. A better way is to count from 20 to 30, pronouncing each syllable aloud without hurrying.

Special Cases

Every rule has its exceptions, and in the case of distant scenery you can often keep your scenes several seconds longer. Landscapes always present so much varied detail, and the eyes need a little time to take it all in.

On the other hand, in a close-up the length of scene can be reduced to about 6 seconds, provided the close-up follows a mid-shot or a general view.

Naturally we are talking about the length of scene as it will be projected, and not in the camera, where the film may have to be run at different speeds.

If the subject is moving very slowly, you can film it at 8 frames a second, and shoot for double the length of time, for example 20 seconds instead of 10. If, on the other hand, it is not possible to dwell on the subject, take it at a higher speed, say 24 or 32 frames, and shorten the taking time correspondingly to compensate for this.

Types of Shots

When you look for the first time through the view-finder of a cine camera, you will be surprised how large the scene appears.

In films, detail plays an important part. You must compel yourself to show your subject in such a way that the details are seen. Which is another way of saying that you must use plenty of close-ups.

In fact, changes of camera distance, as well as angle, is one of the means of bringing life into a motion picture. We are making a film, not presenting a stage play. The camera is not rooted in one spot, so make the most of its mobility.

The main types of shots you will want to use are long-shots, medium shots, and close-ups, while occasionally you may need large close-ups or intermediate shots to put over particular points of the story.

Long Shots

Long-shots serve to establish the surroundings and place the action. In 8 mm., fine detail does not register well, and long-shots must not be overdone. Because details of a long-shot need a longer viewing time, a long shot should always be fairly long—a point you must bear in mind when filming.

104

Medium Shots

A medium shot covers the subject itself. Often this shows full figures, and calls for a taking distance of some 12 to 20 feet.

At this distance the depth of field of the lens takes in a fairly large zone, and focusing is easy. On a focusing type of lens set the mount to 6 metres, or 20 feet. With the lens stopped down to about f 4 or smaller, everything will be sharp from infinity to 10 feet. With a fixed-focus lens, everything is perfectly sharp at these distances.

Use plenty of medium shots in your films; they are suitable nearly always when filming persons, interspersed with close-ups and an occasional long-shot. Don't show the feet of the people on the screen—their faces are far more interesting.

There are various other types of intermediate shots which are given various names by different people. It is part of the charm of the cine camera that the amateur is free to create all sorts of variations upon accepted types of shots.

But on no account shoot your film with people shown full-length all the time, and without the detail of close-ups— that belongs to the old days of "animated pictures".

Close-ups

The close-up is an intimate shot; it shows detail. For close-ups place your subject 4 to 6 feet away from the camera. Naturally this distance is not invariable—it depends also on the actual size of the subject.

Check your focus carefully at this short distance, since the depth of field of the lens is not very great, whether your lens is focusable or fixed focus. Use a good range-finder, then you can focus without disturbing your subject and without attracting his attention—an important matter with children.

The length of a close-up can be less than that of a normal shot—6 to 7 seconds is generally enough.

When filming rapid action the subject will often look more dramatic if it is coming towards the camera. At the same time the picture on the screen will be less blurred.

Large close-ups taken at a distance of 3 feet or less concentrate attention on special detail. Not only must the focus be exact, but you must bear in mind the very limited depth of field.

Such shots should be used only on suitable subjects—when you want to emphasize a significant detail. Generally a large close-up should flash on the screen, and off again, lasting 2-3 seconds.

The long-focus lens (p. 21) is very useful for close-ups. It enables you to work at a greater distance than usual, and may avoid attracting the attention of the subject. This is much the best way to film children, and to catch people unawares.

The long-focus lens needs careful handling; you must

You can follow fast moving subjects by panning the camera round while keeping the main subject in the centre of the field (p. 106).

106

focus accurately since there is little depth of field. At short distances these factors slow down the speed of working. But many subjects cannot be easily filmed in close-up without the long focus lens.

Camera Movements

In addition to changing the camera angle, direction and distance between shots, you can also change them during a take by moving the camera. This often helps to animate an otherwise static scene.

The first essential is that any camera movement must be steady, and not jerky. Otherwise the view will jump about on the screen, which is irritating to the audience. Therefore support the camera on a tripod and use a suitable tripod head for panorama or tilting shots.

Another useful dodge is to film the shot at a high camera speed—provided there is no other action on the scene. This cuts down the time required for the movement, and increases its smoothness. Don't forget to adjust the aperture to allow for the shorter exposure time (p. 72).

The most common camera movement is a horizontal pan (*left*). Always have a close-up at the start and end, and pan slowly. The vertical pan (*right*) is similar in principle. Start from a fixed point in either case. Do not retrace the camera. Use a higher camera-speed than normal to make the movement smoother.

The two main camera movements are change of direction, and change of distance.

You can change direction by tilting the camera vertically up or down, or rotating it horizontally from side to side. The latter is known as panoraming or panning. By means of a tilt or panorama the camera lens can cover a much greater angle, and at the same time present the scene gradually giving the eye time to examine it.

However, don't overdo panoramas; they are apt to become tiring.

The length of a panning shot depends on the lens and filming speed; an average for a 90° panorama would be 30 seconds with a normal lens at 16 f.p.s. Hold the view for 5 seconds before starting the panning, and again for the same length of time at the end.

With long focus lenses allow proportionally longer, and at high camera speeds proportionally less. For instance at 32 f.p.s. you can pan twice as fast as at 16 f.p.s.

Changes of distance are more difficult, as it involves moving the whole camera towards or away from the subject. This so-called tracking is achieved by mounting the camera and tripod on a small platform on wheels or

Straight up and down shots (*left*) yield interesting angles and make a break in a series of otherwise possibly monotonous shots. Hold the camera very firmly. For a tracking shot (*right*) the camera is mounted on a trolley or similar vehicle and moves in on the subject. You may have to change the focus while doing that. Again use a higher taking speed.

Watch the composition of your scene. Don't let the horizon cut the picture in two; either have less than one-third sky (*top left*) or more than two-thirds (*top right*). Use the sky to set off large masses (*bottom*) and this way break up what may otherwise be a monotonous subject.

a similar contrivance. Be careful that the movement is smooth, so don't track over rough ground.

Naturally you must adjust the focus while shooting if you move in close to the subject. So use a small stop for great depth of field, so as to reduce this re-focusing to a minimum.

Variable focus lenses (p. 22) offer a perfect means of producing tracking effects from a fixed position. As you vary the focal length of the lens, the image becomes larger or smaller as if the camera were approaching or receding from the subject.

Filming in Colour

The 8 mm. film size is ideal for colour work. Colour film has practically no grain, and lends itself to projection on quite a large screen without loss of picture quality.

Colour film in 8 mm. is quite cheap—it costs only about half as much again as ordinary panchromatic film.

Colour is easy to handle in 8 mm. because it has the same speed (to within a degree or two) as fine-grain panchromatic film.

In dull weather, without sunshine, colour film gives more brilliant results than black-and-white.

Remember to use the appropriate film for the prevailing light: daylight type films for daylight, and type "A" film with Photofloods. However, if you want to use type A film with daylight, you can place a Wratten 85 filter over the lens. Special flood lamps are available with blue bulbs for use with daylight film. But these expedients are not so efficient as using the correct stock.

Never use mixed lighting; each type of film is balanced for one particular type of light.

With black-and-white film you can always reduce lighting contrasts—for instance in a scene taken by a window—by the addition of Photofloods. But this is not possible with colour film: you would have two dominant colours, or colour casts, and the effect is always unpleasant.

Avoiding Colour Casts

Professional cameramen use a measuring instrument known as a colour temperature meter, and a whole range of colour correcting and compensating filters, to secure accurate colour reproduction—and then don't always achieve it. But the amateur must be content with aiming only at a pleasing reproduction of colours.

A yellow cast may be due to filming early in the morning or late in the evening. Scenes appear unreal, because colours are too emphatic. The only answer is either to tell your audience that such scenes were taken early in the morning or late in the day, or else to cut them out altogether.

A blue cast is a frequent trouble with every type of scene; blue rays are so abundant and the film is not sufficiently compensated to neutralise them, although our eyes are often unaware of them. They can be detected only by a colour temperature meter.

110

Here are some of the causes: a scene taken in the shadow near a window will give a dominant blue, provided the lens stop is correct; this slight dominant tint can be corrected by a light haze filter.

In dull cloudy weather, for distant scenery with a large expanse of sky, and for scenes in shadow, a medium haze filter will neutralise dominant blues rather more fully.

Most people are astonished to find that a dominant blue is strongest on a clear day in open country, mountain views, etc. To compensate for this excess of blue radiation a deeper haze filter is needed.

Hints for Colour

Everything without exception—even the stone of old monuments—gains life when filmed in colour rather than black-and-white.

In dull weather panchromatic film gives a flat image—in colours under the same conditions the result is soft and more pleasing.

Sunshine is not essential to colour: good lighting and the correct lens stop are all you need.

Don't go around looking for subjects to film in colour. Make your colour harmonise with the subject. If you see a flowery bank, don't think of it as a subject for colour—ask yourself whether the colours of the flowers make a pleasant composition.

Close-ups and medium shots give the best results in colour.

Remember always that colour film has a very small latitude of exposure. An error of half a stop will upset your results. A good exposure meter is more than ever necessary.

Filming in Artificial Light

One should not expect too much of wide-aperture lenses. An f 1.5 or f 1.9 lens may help you to get results in bad lighting conditions, with high-speed film, but these results are secured only at the expense of sharpness and depth of field, and in a limited field such as portraiture.

If you intend to do much filming by artificial light arrange to have sufficient lighting to be able to shoot at not too large an aperture.

Photofloods are the most suitable light source. Two types are available: No. 1 and No. 2. The latter consumes 500 watts with an output of 18,000 lumens.

You will need at least two such lamps, and, if the budget permits, three, to be able to film a set, say 6 feet square.

The No. 1 Photoflood is not really satisfactory, and will not give sufficient light on a subject more than 6 feet away.

Your lamps should include reflectors, and they are quite simple to handle.

One useful idea is to mount the lamp or lamps near the camera on a single rod, which is carried in a strong clip. The movable lamp can be put on an adjustable tripod or on a "lazy tongs" support.

These over-run lamps have a life of only about two hours. But it is the sudden switching on of the full current that most quickly causes them to burn out.

You should have an arrangement for pre-heating the filaments, such as a series-parallel switch. The lamps are grouped in pairs, and can be switched either in series for focusing, or in parallel for taking.

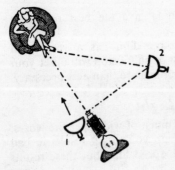

As a simple rule for artificial light set-ups, place one lamp (1) near the camera, and the second lamp (2) to the side so that it is as far from the camera as the latter is from the subject. A third lamp, if available, may be placed behind the subject, shining down at an angle of 45°. The main lamp (1), moves with the camera. (See also p. 109.)

A voltage control system such as a variable transformer also serves to switch on the lamps gradually.

With colour films the lamps must be run at the correct voltage, otherwise the colour of the light may be too blue or too yellow. A Photoflood also gets yellower as it ages, and it is a good idea to keep new lamps for colour filming.

Arranging the Lamps

There is a simple rule for arranging your lamps.

If you have two 500-watt lamps, the first lamp should be placed at the side of the camera, and must move with the camera. The second lamp is placed either on the right or left of the camera, at the apex of an imaginary right-angled isosceles triangle, one side of which is the line from the camera to the subject.

If you can run to a third lamp, put it *behind* the subject, on the opposite side from the second lamp, illuminating the subject from above. Keep it a little off-centre so that the light does not shine into the lens.

When you are shooting on colour film, it is better to do without the second lamp, or to place it near the first lamp. This arrangement reduces the lighting contrast, which must be kept down in colour, and also increases the amount of light available for filming.

The Stop to Use

When using an exposure table intended for cine work, allow only for the principal lamp—that placed near the camera. Modelling and effect lamps should not be taken into account.

With an ordinary exposure meter measure the light on your hand, placed in front of the subject, and then open up one stop more than is indicated. This is a necessary precaution, for your hand reflects more light than the rest of the scene.

Better still, measure the brightness of a key tone (p. 77),

113

held in front of the subject, when you can use the aperture actually shown, without correction.

With an incident light meter, the opal cap over the cell is held in front of the subject, but pointing towards the camera.

Remember always that the stop must be altered if the distance from the principal lamp to the subject is changed.

Informal Shooting

When you set about taking some shots of children or the family don't waste too much time in preliminaries, which are likely to mar the spontaneity and naturalness of the scene. Don't aim at the production methods of the professional cinema.

The best family films are taken quite simply, by letting the people or children do just what they like. The set must be flooded with sufficient light to simplify focusing and to give you ample depth of field.

Indoors you may have to content yourself with mid-shots and close-ups, unless you have a wide-angle lens or attachment. Always use a lens hood.

114

Subjects for 8 mm. Films

YOU are now ready to tackle almost any normal subject. But before you do, bear in mind a few general hints.

Make sure that your scenes tie up with each other. They must have continuity; don't just shoot animated lantern slides joined together, with no connection between them.

The best place to learn how to construct your film is at the cinema. A number of scenes representing consecutive action form a sequence; the end of a sequence may be marked by a fade-out—i.e., the scene gets darker until it is completely black.

Remember always that close-ups are more important than general views. But at short distances, keep your attention on the distance setting. Use an accurate range-finder for distances down to a couple of feet, or failing this, a tape-measure.

Travel

The travel film is the amateur's classical subject. The length of your film will, of course, depend on the distance and importance of your journey.

When going abroad with a foreign-made camera carry a receipt from the shop where you bought the camera and equipment, to avoid complications when you return. Otherwise you may have to pay duty and purchase tax.

Here are a few subjects for the opening scenes: final preparations—packing your trunks—pasting on labels—loading up the taxi. Include also maps showing your route.

These and similar scenes can be filmed before you go or after your return.

Instead of sub-titles, film a sign-post showing the name of

the country or the town. If you are going abroad, get a globe, spin it and put your finger on one point, as if you had made your choice by chance.

Try to avoid "postcard views"—look out for local curiosities: views of old houses, shops, queer methods of locomotion, historic monuments. Avoid scenes that are conventional or too familiar.

If you have a long-focus lens, emphasise details of architecture, advertisements, windows, iron-work. Use a long-focus lens, too, for filming the inhabitants—they will be less self-conscious and your pictures may be more original.

In foreign countries don't use your camera on troops or police, or on military buildings.

Try to avoid the use of a wide-angle lens. It is better to move your camera backwards very slowly while shooting.

Don't forget to show close-ups among your scenery.

It is rarely wise to film a moving vehicle, but if you must, shoot at 24 or 32 frames. It is better to shoot standing up if you have an open car.

If people are included in your picture, don't let them take up stiff and conventional attitudes.

For the end film the back of a train, and fade out on the words "The End". Or you could take a general view of a station from a bridge, with smoke effects. (This could, of course, equally well serve as the start of your film.)

Check your equipment some weeks before you leave. Make some tests of your exposure meter. If your journey is particularly important, take a spare exposure meter.

When travelling abroad, have your equipment checked at the frontiers; it will save you trouble later on.

Bring back a few picture postcards to serve as backgrounds to your titles.

Holidays

This is the subject most widely filmed by amateurs, but still the most popular.

116

Don't film the obvious things—go after humorous scenes.

With a long-focus lens you can catch people unawares.

Colour is not essential—a good black-and-white film can be equally interesting.

Holiday films generally resolve themselves into a series of sequences each dealing with a particular subject. Each such sequence must be carefully subtitled.

Your film should show all your holiday activities, from a quiet nap to local excursions.

A lot of holiday filming includes travel scenes. Again film all the preparations, loading up the luggage, trace out the route on a map. Then go on to a few shots of your departure, a stop *en route* for lunch. Views of the locality, of the hotel or restaurant.

Other shots that will suggest themselves are scenes of local life, ancient houses, the old church, crucifixes, with cloud effects. Get a take of people coming out of church on Sunday (a long-focus lens will prevent them looking self-conscious). You might get a story of the local fair. Check up your history, but don't be tedious.

During the holiday, picnics, visits, fishing—or forty winks in the shade or on the beach—will make suitable sequences.

The passage of time can be indicated by a moving shadow of a tree.

End your film with a sunset, or some scene to suggest your regret at the end of the holiday.

Send your films to your usual dealer for processing, if possible as soon as they are exposed. Try not to send the whole lot at once—if you can see what you have already shot you have the chance of adjusting your taking conditions.

Children

By clever editing you can create an altogether original film—a film which in a few reels will show scenes taken over a number of years. You can, for instance, pick out

sequences dealing with a single member of the family—
from the time of his birth to his schooldays, his holidays,
his sports and amusements. Or you can take as a theme a
single day in a child's life, from the time he gets up to the
time he goes to bed.

Children grow very quickly—a couple of hundred feet of
film every three months is not too much for the tiny ones.

Introductory material can be replaced by a pleasing title.
You might start with the child in bed; he wakes up (actually
you must shoot this during the day when he is thoroughly
awake), followed by dressing and washing; a stroll or indoor
games. Go on to the midday meal (bring in close-ups of
the various courses), the afternoon nap—until he wakes up,
and goes for a walk. Film the evening meal and bed-time,
with a long-shot of parents around his cot. End by the
bedroom lights being turned out.

Keep to close-ups. If necessary you can film interiors
near the window.

In editing, don't run your scenes too long; keep any over-
matter for other films.

Take care of the lighting, and don't expose a young child
too long before the camera. A film such as this will need
several sittings.

Don't forget in your titles and sub-titles to indicate the
date and place, and note any special events.

Weddings

Try to avoid conventional views and scenes that look like
posed portraits. Strive for originality and movement.

Always obtain permission to film within the church or
register office in advance from the clergyman or registrar.

The maximum length of your film should be twenty
minutes.

You will need fast film for shots which will have to be
taken in poor lighting conditions.

Start off with last-minute preparations in the kitchen or
reception hall, and shots of the family. Then follow with

shots of the arrival of the bouquet, the arrival of the guests—
shots of the presents, the bride's dress, and the bride
leaving with her father. All these should be short takes
lasting 5 seconds or less.

Dissolve to the arrival at the church (the groom has
perhaps been kept waiting). Take shots of the ceremony
if the lighting permits, and in the vestry.

When the people are coming out of church, film the
family groups arranging themselves. Try to find some
humorous touch, avoid conventional poses. Don't shoot
while everybody is standing still for the photographer.

Other scenes should include the wedding breakfast, the
menu, the guests—not forgetting if possible the cook, some
decorative dishes. Don't forget the ceremony of cutting
the cake. If conditions permit take some shots of the
guests after the meal, perhaps in the garden.

Conclude with the happy couple driving off; fade-out
on the car disappearing in the distance.

Study in advance as far as possible the various places
where you will have to work, and look out for suitable
camera angles.

For interiors, check the mains before connecting up your
lamps—it is hardly a suitable time to blow a fuse!

In editing, avoid too long scenes, and don't forget the
close-ups, which can, if necessary, be made after the
ceremony and so fill any possible gaps.

Filming a Cruise

This is a vast subject, and always contains plenty of
material just right for filming.

Use colour for preference—colour always adds interest
to the subject—but don't mix colour and black-and-white.

Try not to use different emulsions; for instance high
speed and fine-grain, or warm-toned emulsion, together
with the ordinary blue-black tones.

When you land in port, don't forget the customs form-
alities before leaving.

119

When you build up your story, include general views of the harbour and of the boat, the embarkation of passengers and loading of the luggage. Take a few amusing shots of people coming on board.

Don't miss the effect of the ship's whistle signalling the departure.

As the ship leaves the quay, get some scenes of the various things that are going on on board (these shots can be taken during the voyage).

As you leave each port of call, include a few feet of the quays and harbour, for purposes of record.

Avoid conventional scenes reminiscent of picture post-cards—strive for originality and make use of your long-focus lens.

Don't overdo highly coloured scenes.

Concentrate on local points of interest—shops, old houses, markets, itinerant salesmen. Don't overdo old monuments.

If you are travelling in a party, try not to include too many people whom you will probably never meet again.

Make a point of filming scenes of everyday life aboard ship. But wait a few days before starting on these shots, so that you will get to know the geography of the ship. Include a few typical scenes, such as an officer plotting the course on a chart.

Sunrise and sunset make attractive shots, with parties of your fellow travellers in the foreground.

Scenes of waves breaking on the beach, or distant mountains with sky effects, get a little monotonous, even if it is some famous mountain or an extinct volcano.

Do not miss scenes of passengers going ashore, surrounded by natives offering their wares. A long-focus lens is useful here.

Take some typical scenes of late arrivals, to cut in with the whistle of the departing ship.

Finish your film quickly with a long-shot of a harbour or the ship's wake.

Organizing the Story

Think over some titles during the voyage; signposts and street names can be used in place of sub-titles to recall the places visited.

Always mark your scenes and the rolls of film to assist you in editing; some wording photographed on to the film is far better than notes written on the cartons.

Your film will generally be too long—cut out any unnecessary footage.

Most people tend to use up their stock extravagantly at first, with the result that they run short of stock before the end of the voyage. Your film should form a general souvenir of the voyage, and not of the details of embarkation and disembarkation, or long dreary scenes of one country to the exclusion of another.

If your film starts in colour, continue it in colour to the end, notwithstanding bad weather. Generally speaking, if your exposure is correct, a shot in colour will always look more interesting than in black-and-white.

If you are travelling in hot countries, remember that although your films may be in tropical packing, they are not protected against heat. Try to prevent them becoming overheated as this can result in loss of speed.

Other Subjects

We have covered a few examples of 8 mm. films, but they are, of course, far from exhaustive.

In time you will want to film more ambitious stories, real or fictional. At this stage you have to start planning your film.

The key to the job is the idea. Once you have got an idea or plot for a film—and it need not be a complicated one by any means—write it down in the form of a simple story. Then convert the story into a shooting script.

The script is in fact your real plan for shooting the film. There you list each incident, every stage of your story, in terms of a film scene. Note down the type of shot—whether long shot, medium shot, or close-up—and the approximate length of the take. Develop your story so that each take brings out a significant point of it.

You will learn a great deal about the art of scripting from a visit to your local cinema. There you will see how each scene links up with the next one so that you have a continuous flow of action or presentation. Examine your own script in the light of a professional motion picture. See whether it presents the story as smoothly and at a suitable pace.

Then settle down to filming the individual takes. They need not be taken in the order in which they appear in the shooting script, you can always join them up in the required sequence later on.

While the shooting script is a valuable plan of operations, it need not be a rigid one. You can always have second thoughts during filming, but the important thing is that you are working to a plan, and thus cutting out a great deal of waste.

Tricks and Special Effects

IT adds to the interest of your film and avoids monotony if you cut in various special effects or well chosen trick shots.

Various types of trick shots are classified in the following tables. Most of them can be carried out with the simplest of cameras. Advanced types of cameras, full of gadgets, naturally give you more scope, especially those fitted with reverse action.

Needless to say, this list of trick effects is by no means complete; you will no doubt be able to think up others.

I. APERTURE EFFECTS

Effect	Result on Projection	How Obtained	Remarks and Hints
Fade-in	Starting from darkness, the scene gradually lightens to full brightness.	Start taking at the smallest stop—open up gradually to the normal stop.	For this effect you must cover a range of 3 or 4 stops to allow for compensation in processing.
Fade-out	The normal picture gradually darkens until it almost disappears.	Towards the end of the scene close the iris gradually to the smallest stop.	As above.
Lap Dissolve	The first scene gradually disappears while the following scene gradually appears at the same rate.	Finish the first scene with a fade-out. Put the cap on the lens, run the film back for the length of the fade. Take the cap off the lens, film the next scene, gradually opening the iris.	This effect is possible only with a camera fitted with reverse wind. The camera must be on a tripod. The effect may be spoilt by compensation in processing.

II. FOCUS EFFECTS

Effect	Result on Projection	How obtained	Remarks and Hints
Focus-in	At first there is nothing on the screen then the picture gradually appears and gets sharper until it is in correct focus.	Set the focus to the shortest distance—say 2 ft. or less. While the film is running, turn the focus ring slowly, stopping at the correct distance for the subject.	Best used on close-ups. The effect is quite easy, and cannot be upset in processing.
Focus-out	The normal picture gradually goes out of focus until there is just a blur.	At the end of the scene gradually focus the lens forward as far as it will go, then stop the motor.	These two effects may be combined for instance to change from one person to another.

III. USING ATTACHMENTS ON THE LENS

Effect	Result on Projection	How Obtained	Remarks and Hints
Over-filtering	Moonlight or night effect.	Use an orange or red filter, underexpose considerably. Choose a sheet of water reflecting the sun.	A realistic moonlight effect impossible to obtain actually at night.
Multiple Images	The same scene (preferably a close-up) is seen in duplicate, triplicate or quintuplicate, each image performing the same action.	Fit a prismatic lens with 2, 3, or 5 facets. Sometimes this lens can be rotated.	Very amusing effect after a good dinner or a few drinks. Open up half a stop.

Effect	Result on Projection	How Obtained	Remarks and Hints
Fog and Mist	Misty image — the subject appears from a thick fog.	Use a special fog filter. Choose your subject and background with care. Under-expose half a stop.	It is difficult to film actually in the fog, and the effect can be obtained best by the use of filters.
Wipe	A black mask gradually moves across the screen blotting out the picture. Conversely, the mask moves off the screen, revealing the picture.	An opaque shutter is gradually moved across the field of the lens. The same shutter is gradually moved out of the lens field.	A wipe serves to change from one scene to another. The effect is not altered during developing as are fade-outs.
Framing or Vignetting the image	A black mask surrounds part of the image as if it were viewed through binoculars.	A mask with a suitable opening is placed some distance from the lens, connected to it by bellows.	Key-hole and other shapes may be obtained in the same manner.

IV. USING OPTICAL SYSTEMS

Effect	Result on Projection	How Obtained	Remarks and Hints
Wide-angle (widening the field of the lens)	The image covers a field twice as wide as with a lens of normal focus.	Fit a wide-angle attachment to the lens, giving a field twice as wide. No change in iris.	The only way to secure wide-angle effects, as lenses of less than 12.5 mm. focus are unusual.

Effect	Result on Projection	How Obtained	Remarks and Hints
Long-focus (reduction of lens field)	The effect is the same as with a lens of twice the normal focal length.	Fit a suitable optical system giving a magnification of 2, with consequent reduction in the camera.	Suitable for cameras with non-interchangeable lenses.
Tracking or "zoom" shots.	The camera appears to move upwards or away from the subject.	Use a variable-focus lens.	Capable of rapid tracking or "zoom" shots.

V. TRICKS WITH THE MOTOR

Effect	Result on Projection	How Obtained	Remarks and Hints
Slow motion	All the movements of the subject are slowed down.	Use the highest speed of 64 frames a second.	Increase lens stop proportionately. This speed is suitable for filming persons or vehicles in rapid motion.
Semi-rapid	The slowing down of movement is less marked.	Failing a 64-frame speed, use the next speed, generally 32 frames.	For filming persons or vehicles in motion.
Smooth pan	When the camera is panned rapidly it is better to use the 24-frame speed.	Use the 24-frame speed to obtain even movement.	This speed should always be used with panning shots.

126

Effect	Result on Projection	How Obtained	Remarks and Hints
Accelerated movement	Movement is speeded up, people walk quickly.	Use the 8-frame speed.	Do not use this taking speed too often—not always pleasing in projection. Suitable for titles; for bad lighting condition.
Stop-action	Letters move to form a title—a plant grows visibly.	Use the single-frame movement.	Avoid differences in exposure between frames.
Appearances, disappearances, ghosts.	For conjuring effects.	Stop the motor, change the subject, resume shooting.	Don't use too often.

VI. TRICKS ON THE FILM

Effect	Result on Projection	How Obtained	Remarks and Hints
Tinting	Blue tinting for night effects—red for sunset.	Mordanting and dyeing after the film is processed.	Needs care, but gives pleasing effects on suitable subjects.
Chemical fade	Fade-in or fade-out, superior to those done on the iris.	Use black dye specially made for the purpose. Feed the end of the film inch by inch into the dye—the longer the film is in the dye the more opaque it becomes.	Absolute cleanliness is essential. This inexpensive method enables fades to be inserted as desired.

Effect	Result on Projection	How Obtained	Remarks and Hints
Chemical wipes	Same as camera wipes, but produced after taking and processing.	Cut stencils in adhesive tape, stick on to the film, paint the film with black dye. When the tape is removed those parts covered by it are not dyed.	Apply the dye with a brush—the results are neater.
Wipes by adhesive tape	A useful method of changing from scene to scene.	Strips of opaque adhesive tape with suitable designs are applied to the desired sections of the film.	The best way to obtain wipe effects on a film already processed. Easy to do and lasts indefinitely.

Titling Your Films

THERE is no need to ask why films should be titled. A title and sub-titles are absolutely indispensable in the veriest of amateur films.

A title is as important to a film as to a book or a picture. But many amateurs neglect this point, and present their films untitled thus losing the "finishing" touch.

The Main Title

The main title must be brief. In three words or so it must acquaint your audiences with the subject matter of the film. It must be carefully photographed, with some touch of originality inspired by the subject of the film. It may include a date.

Your main title at least may be prepared by laboratories specialising in such work, who have at their disposal a wide range of lettering, and ideas on presentation.

Sub-titles

Sub-titles serve to tie together the various sequences. They explain the action, establish the location, and, when necessary, indicate the dialogue.

A spoken commentary may replace titles, but well executed titles at the right points in your film give it a finished appearance. Titles may seem unimportant, but they do much to enhance the presentation of your film.

Sub-titles must be quite short and to the point. A long title becomes tedious, especially in the middle of a film.

A title must be explicit, and sketches may be used to reduce the number of words.

A sub-title, even on a serious subject, should not be boring. It can be quite amusing, ornamented by sketches.

One thing that you should avoid in your sub-titles is many dialogue titles, so popular in the days of the silent films. Such titles slow down the action. It is far better to try to shoot your film so that the actions speak for themselves, and so avoid unnecessary commentaries.

Discursive sub-titles are out of place in the amateur film. If your film deals with a foreign country, don't make your audiences read through a title lifted straight out of the guide book. Whether they are members of your own family or of your club, your audiences have not come to be instructed by your film, but to be amused, and to share in your own pleasure.

The opposite style, the telegraphic style, is equally unsuitable. But it is better to use no titles at all than to show your film with hurriedly prepared titling.

The End Title

Your film must finish with the words THE END, or just END. But don't use an "End" title of the sort that can be bought by the foot; it should be written in the same style as your other titles.

A touch of fantasy is sometimes suitable to finish a film. If you make your titles yourself, it is quite easy to animate these three letters, using the large letters made for display purposes.

Your end title may fade in, and should always be faded out. Your signature as the maker of the film may be worked into the design.

Make the fade-out yourself by closing down the lens (p. 123), or a processing laboratory can do it for you.

Direct Titles

Sub-titles can be made while you are shooting your film; it is indeed a sound idea to make a point of doing so. Titles produced in this fashion are often the most interesting, the most alive, and the easiest for your audiences to follow. They are, incidentally, the most economical.

Numerous titles can be filmed directly in the camera. For example, in a travel film, destination boards may locate the action. A station name, especially if it is in a distinctive style, gives your audience an idea of the country.

A coloured poster makes an excellent sub-title for a football match, a village fair, or a bull-fight.

Mile-posts and A.A. and R.A.C. notices will indicate the number of miles you have travelled, or the height of the road. There are innumerable such examples.

Handbills distributed by the railway companies and travel agencies can be used to show where you are going for a holiday.

A route card shows without an unnecessary word the route you are taking. At a stopping point, a reading glass serves to make the name of the locality readable to everybody. This effect is easily carried out with your normal lens, which may, however, need re-focusing.

Filming Direct Titles

All these examples can be filmed with your ordinary lens, or possibly with a supplementary lens. If you have a focusing lens, it must be capable of focusing down to about 20 inches.

Focus with the utmost care when working at these short distances of less than a yard. A reliable rangefinder is useful.

Distances should be measured from the front of the lens, or of the supplementary lens if used, although in practice it is near enough to measure from the front of the camera when working in the open air and in good light.

If your lens is of the fixed focus type, you will not be able to work at short distances without the aid of a supplementary lens. In any case, two or three such lenses should form part of your kit (p. 91).

For variable focus lenses a supplementary lens of 3 diopters will enable you to go down to a foot, giving a large close-up when you need it.

But for making titles in daylight, you can generally shoot at a distance of a yard or more.

To find the correct lens aperture, it is best to make use of the key tone method (p. 77), or of an exposure meter of the incident light type (p. 76).

Always work closely enough for the lettering on the card to be readable in your finder.

Never tilt your camera in order to cover the whole of a long title card; you will make it difficult to read.

If your title is important, first show all of it, then take close-ups of any names which need to be stressed.

Your audiences want to read your titles—in the case of the more important ones keep the footage long enough to give them plenty of time.

Always use a tripod for making titles if you have no titling bench. But if you have to work in the wind, or on a tripod that is not too steady, shoot at a higher speed, say 32 frames, so that your titles will look steady.

Framing Parallax

Remember to allow for parallax, due to the fact that the viewfinder axis does not coincide with that of the lens. Your viewfinder should be adjusted for working at an average distance of say 12 feet. If you are shooting at a shorter distance of say 3 feet, always make allowance for parallax—in other words, don't place your subject exactly in the centre of the viewfinder field, but a short distance off the centre, in the direction of the lens.

You may also have to make allowance in height if your finder is mounted on top of the camera, as in the majority of cameras.

In many finders, there are one or two additional frames which indicate the limits at shorter distances.

132

Titlers

If you want to make your own titles methodically and accurately you must have a titler.

This is a support carrying the camera perpendicularly above the title card. You will need in addition some lights, and supplementary lenses.

Given these basic requirements, a titler can be quite simple, although there are various designs.

A good steady tripod makes quite a good titler. Mount your camera on the tilting head, with its lens pointing downwards—that is to say, with the optical axis perpendicular to the title card. Centre the card either by means of a plumb-line, or better still a suitable aligning rod.

One such aligning rod can be screwed into a filter mount and placed in front of the lens to indicate the optical axis, and so facilitate the exact centring of the card. Simply place the point of the rod in the exact centre of the title. The rod may also give measurements of lens-to-title distances. This accessory is useful not only for titles, but also whenever you are using a supplementary lens.

If you own an enlarger for still negatives, you can easily convert it by adapting the arm carrying the lamp-house to support the camera. Probably the manufacturer can

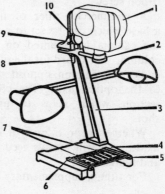

A simple vertical titler with its own lighting unit will cover all the needs of the average amateur. The camera (1) is mounted on the top of the column (3). The camera is centred and aligned by the controls (8), (9), and (10), and set for close-up work with the help of the supplementary lens (2). The title card (5) is held in guides (6) on the baseboard, and aligned against the stops (7).

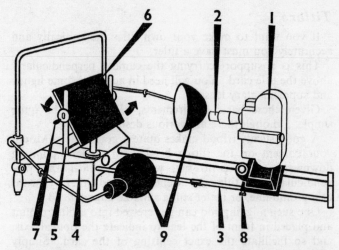

A more elaborate titler includes various refinements. The camera (1), fitted with a suitable close-up attachment (2), moves along a twin rail (3), and can be clamped in any position by the screw (8). This is necessary when the titler is used vertically. The title base (4), carries the title frame (5) or other support for the title (6). In this case a flap-over control (7) is provided for changing. The lamps (9) are fully adjustable in any direction and angle.

supply a bracket on which you can fix the camera by the tripod screw.

A commercial titler of up-to-date design consists of a base which can be set to work vertically or horizontally; the camera is mounted on a bracket sliding along the column. The board for the title card is placed at the farther end of this column, opposite the camera and perpendicular to the optical axis. The column is generally of square section, which helps in producing tracking or zoom shots.

Whether your titler is a commercial model or home-made, you will always need supplementary lenses (p. 91) and lights.

For titling, supplementary lenses of 2 and 3 diopters are

needed. These two lenses can if necessary be used together, but you will have to stop down considerably to neutralise distortion of the edges of the picture.

Rigidity is the first essential of a titler; it should not be too light, because the camera motor may vibrate when running.

There must be no play in the camera bracket as it slides along the column, otherwise tracking shots will be impossible—the titles will go out of centre.

A titler must be carefully made if your titles are to be central. A poorly framed title is a bad title.

Title Letters

For lettering you can use drawn letters or movable letters of plastic, cork or felt.

Cork letters are quite inexpensive, and are strong enough to stand up to repeated use. But always handle them carefully, preferably with tweezers.

Letters and figures can be obtained in different sizes, capitals and lower-case letters, roman and italics. For making titles in colour, they can easily be coloured by means of lacquer paint, or even water-colours. Cork letters can, of course, be used only in a vertical titler.

Plastic letters are easier to handle. They are made in two types: one with a spike at the back for fixing to a title board, and another type with an adhesive surface.

Felt letters are obtainable in white, in capitals and lower-case italics. They must be used on a cloth or velvet background, to which they stick, but can be easily taken off.

Separate plastic title letters are in many ways simplest to use. They carry a spike at the back for fixing to a vertical or horizontal background.

135

They are rather more difficult to handle, but can be used in many combinations with other types of letters.

Lighting

If your titler is used on a balcony or in the garden, or even near the window, daylight may be adequate. However, the light may change while you are working, and it is difficult to create certain effects with diffused light. It is far better to use a couple of Photofloods.

These should preferably be of the reflector type, which are easily handled and not too cumbersome. The reflector gives a sharply and uniformly lit area. Two Photofloods No. 1 placed one each side of the camera are quite enough.

To obtain relief effects on the letters, a small spotlight may be useful, set at a low angle.

Setting up the Title

There are practically no fixed rules for titling your films or for making titles. Everybody has his own ideas, his own peculiarities. This is what gives amateur cinematography its charm. But there are a few essential rules which will prevent you wasting time and film.

The centring of the camera and the title card is the most important job; the slightest error will put the title noticeably out of centre or out of square. Your titler must hold the camera absolutely rigidly.

On the title board, draw the two diagonals, then if the centre of a plumb-line from the lens (on a vertical titler) or of an aligning rod, is placed at their intersection, you will be sure that the board is central.

Check this by running off a few inches of film on a sheet of squared paper centred on the title board. This will at the same time show you the field of your lens. After this test is processed, project it, when you will see easily whether the title card is central, and also what width of margin you have to allow.

The titler is then ready for use. The position of the camera must be precisely fixed, otherwise you will have to start all over again.

Effect Titles

Your main and end titles should have fade-ins and fade-outs. For sub-titles a fade-out is enough.

When several titles follow one another it is a good idea to dissolve from one to the next, provided your camera has a reverse drive.

An effect of movement and relief is quite easily obtained by moving the spotlight so as to cast a long moving shadow.

A title of letters appearing one after the other, or disappearing in the same way, can be produced by running at 8 f.p.s. or single-frame. But when you film frame by frame, the exposure is apt to vary between frames, producing an unpleasant flicker in projection, and quite ruining the effect.

Long titles moving upwards are quite easy to make with a vertical titler. Simply arrange a couple of guides through which you can slowly pull a long strip of paper.

A swinging title is equally simple. There must be a space underneath the title card, and the card must be pivoted so that it can turn upon its centre line.

On the same pivot, a drum may be mounted, carrying lettering around its surface.

The various types of effect title include the flap-over (*left*) consisting of a pivoted board which turns over from one side to the other; the rotating title (*centre left*) mounted on a drum; the shutter wipe (*centre right*) and the travelling title for long texts, which move across the field of view (*right*).

A tracking or zoom shot is made by sliding the camera very slowly towards or away from the title card. In the former case the title will gradually get larger on the screen, in the second it will appear to move away and get smaller. A tracking shot calls for a precision type titler, because it is quite difficult to slide the camera without jerkiness and without getting it out of alignment. In many titlers of older design there is appreciable play in the camera support as soon as the clamping screw is loosened.

For film stock use an ultra-fine grain type.

Backgrounds and Timing

The background of your titles is quite important. The usual type is white or light-coloured lettering on a black background; reading is then easier than with the opposite arrangement, which is not recommended.

The background can be replaced by a photograph or, for instance, a route card. In this case, arrange for the lettering to come over a darker part of the background.

To work out the length of titles, stick to the following rule. When the film is projected at normal speed you must be able to read it one-and-a-half times, because you know the text. If on projection you find the title is too short, it is always possible to slow down at that moment, or if it is too long, speed up the projector. But that is an emergency measure, for not many projectors have adjustable speeds.

If you cannot make your own titles, get out your wording and pass it over at a firm specialising in such work. Don't let your films be seen without titles.

Editing

BEFORE you show your films to your public, they must be edited. This consists in assembling the shots in logical order, after cutting out poor shots or uninteresting scenes. You can also add shots made after the original production, together with titles and sub-titles.

Editing is a most important operation. It is editing that imparts rhythm to your film. You should have proper equipment to carry out the various operations conveniently and comfortably, otherwise editing becomes a difficult task, instead of a continuation of the pleasure of shooting.

Planning the Job

When your film arrives back from the processing station, it will be in the form of a single-eight film, wound on an aluminium spool.

First view it to discover just what shots each reel contains, and number the reels in the order in which they were taken.

Next, index the scenes to help you in cutting. Write on the packing of each reel the titles of the various scenes.

Then separate the various scenes (cutting out any black or blurred frames or noting them for retakes) and wind them into small rolls, head out. They can be kept in small boxes, such as pill boxes, or in the pigeon-holes of an editing table.

Sets of pigeon-holes can be obtained, each compartment intended to hold one scene or one small roll of film. These special racks can be quite well replaced by small numbered boxes.

So, cut your film into scenes, or if more convenient,

several short scenes together, and place each roll in its compartment.

Jot down on paper a list of the subjects in each compartment which are available.

Points of Film Editing

You will have your own ideas on how to arrange and present your films—there are few fixed rules. The vital point is that the theme of the film must be developed and followed, by means of pictures and titles.

The tempo, or speed of action, can be modified—purposely or otherwise—by the length of your scenes.

The various stages of editing once you have your scenes separated are as follows:

1. Insert titles and sub-titles, putting them first into the correspondingly numbered compartments.

2. Before joining the sections together, make a final check on the viewer (p. 141), or by a magnifying glass, to see that the scenes follow on correctly.

3. Join the various scenes together on the splicer (p. 141). As the scenes are joined, wind the film up on the right-hand winder head (p. 142).

4. Join on to the beginning of the film a long leader of undeveloped film, on which you can write the title of your film.

5. At the other end join another leader—but not of the same unexposed film as the first leader.

6. Always wind *emulsion out*.

Animated Viewers

With 8 mm. film an animated viewer is really essential for comfortable editing.

The viewer shows a moving picture on a tiny screen. The mechanical system is not the same as in a projector (p. 150): the film runs continuously, and an animated picture is

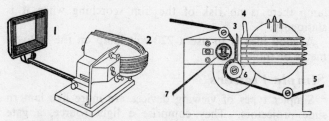

A typical animated viewer usually consists of some kind of miniature projection screen (1) and a projector unit (2). This incorporates a gate with pressure plate (3), a punch (4), to mark any particular point on the film itself, and a sprocket (6) driving an optical shutter system (7), which takes the place of the intermittent transport. The film (5) usually comes from one of the reels on the editing table, and is wound up on another reel.

obtained by means of a rotating optical system driven by the film itself. The viewer also incorporates a small lamp and a projection system.

The purchase of a viewer merits as much attention as of your projector. Don't forget that your film is something unique, and you must examine carefully all the components comprising a viewer.

The gate through which the film runs, either with or without a pressure plate, must be so constructed that it cannot scratch your film.

It is the film, or rather its perforations, that drive the optical system. This system must therefore run smoothly, and be well balanced so that it will place no strain upon the film.

Viewers sometimes incorporate a footage counter for the film. This counter should show the length of film, as well as the number of frames.

A film punch is a useful feature; you can punch the film to the exact frame, which makes it easier to find later.

The projector also makes an excellent viewer but is a little inconvenient to handle during editing. All you have to do is to replace the usual projection lamp by a low-powered lamp, possibly of 100 watts. With such a lamp there is no risk of the film scorching when it is stationary.

A good idea is to use a 220-volt lamp on the 110-volt mains or transformer.

Simple Viewers

Simpler types of viewing devices are more like lantern slide projectors. They comprise a light source, a gate through which the film runs, a punch, a small projection lens, and a ground-glass screen which is hooded to make the picture easier to examine. The picture is visible only when the film is stationary behind the aperture.

This type of viewer is quite useful, but it is less practicable than the animated viewer. It is good enough when you only want to identify and assemble scenes, but it is impossible to judge from it the quality of the picture, and you may find yourself continually turning to your projector.

A magnifying glass is of use only for identifying scenes, but not suitable for judging detail in the tiny frames of 8 mm. film.

Rewinders

It is inconvenient to unwind and wind up a reel by hand during editing. You will therefore want some form of mechanical winder.

For 8 mm. film a pair of winders to carry 400 feet spools will be quite sufficient. The winder to your left should preferably have some form of brake.

You can buy rewinders already mounted on a base. But it is generally better to buy separate heads, and to mount them on your bench, or on a plank of suitable length.

If fixed to the bench, they will be rigid, and this will allow your left hand to be free when working. Another point is that it is often useful to place a viewer or a splicer between the two heads, and generally these are of different size.

The right-hand winder head with which you will do

most of the winding up should be geared up, in order to save time in winding.

Splicers

This is an accessory for quickly and accurately joining two lengths of film together. Ideally, you should buy one with the projector—a film may break at any moment. Even the best of splices may fail before or during projection.

To make a join or splice with the splicer, proceed as follows:

1. Place the ends of the two films to be joined in the splicer, register them by pins which engage with the perforations, and clamp them in position.

2. Cut the two ends—the splicer automatically makes an accurate cut. If you examine the two ends you will find that the right-hand film is cut *beyond* the perforation, while the left-hand film is cut just *before* one. These two ends of film are the sections that will be lapped over one another and welded together.

A splicer (*left*) consists of three hinged plates (2), (3), and a fixed plate (8), mounted on a base (4) which may be screwed to the bench by the holes (5). The film is laid on the register pins (11), (12) and held down by the plate (9), while the scraper (6) on a movable arm (7), removes the emulsion layer. The other film strip is held between (2) and (3), clipped together by the catch (1). A trimming edge (10) is usually incorporated. Multi-gauge splicers have locating pins for each of the film sizes on the baseboard (*right*).

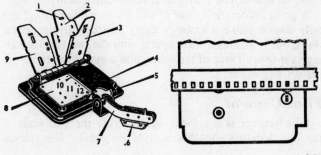

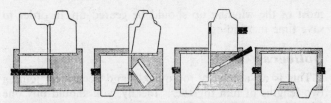

To splice two lengths of film, place the first piece emulsion side up on the baseplate, and clamp down (*left*). Scrape off the emulsion right down to the film base (*centre left*). Some splicers have built-in scrapers. Trim the other film end and fit it between the double hinged plates. Apply film cement to the scraped portion (*centre right*). Bring down the hinged plates with the second piece of film, and lock (*right*). This trims the surplus film off the first piece, and presses both pieces firmly together. Leave for 10-20 seconds, to let the cement set.

3. By means of the scraper remove the thin layer of emulsion from the tiny piece of film that is exposed, scraping down to the base.

4. By means of a small brush or a glass rod, apply just a touch of film cement to this narrow strip.

5. *Immediately* press the other piece of film, which you have already cut, on to the cemented portion; this must be done mechanically and quickly, as the cement will rapidly evaporate.

6. Apply pressure to the two ends (either by your finger or automatically) for about 10 seconds.

7. Raise the clamps gently and lift the film. The joint should hold firmly, but you must still handle the film carefully, otherwise you may pull it out of alignment.

A good automatic splicer is well worth while getting; not only does it make it easier to carry out the various operations, but it assures a clean splice, with the two films adhering over the full area of the splice, and—most important—in perfect alignment.

Film Cement

Film cement is a solvent which welds the two ends of the film together, just like a weld in metal. The cement serves simply to soften and partly dissolve the base in order to facilitate the weld.

Films nowadays do not have the same base as during the war years, and the favourite cement which you used in those days is not suitable for modern film stock. Only by using good cement can you rely upon your splices. Every film manufacturer supplies cement specially suited to his film base.

Always buy film cement in small quantities; in normal use a tiny bottle will do thousands of joins.

It is easy to upset the bottle, and the cement will evaporate quickly, so it is a good idea to keep only a very small quantity of cement in the bottle you are working from, with a brush fixed in the cork. The rest of the cement is kept in store, and will not deteriorate so quickly when it is not periodically uncorked.

An Editing Table

Every cine worker has his own ideas on the layout of his editing table. The arrangement of the accessories is generally the same, but their number varies according to the importance of the job. Here are some suggestions.

In front of you is the animated viewer. On each side are the two winder heads, so mounted that the film runs in line, since it is the winder that draws the film through the viewer. The splicer is fixed to the right of the viewer, out of line with the film path.

Right and left of the splicer are two receptacles. One serves for the film cement. Some people also like to have a drop of water handy, since the film scrapes more easily when it is moistened.

Finally, within easy reach are the pigeon-holes or boxes with the rolls of film.

You will find it more convenient to load the projector if your spools, whether aluminium or plastic, have the three driving slots in each cheek, so that they are reversible.

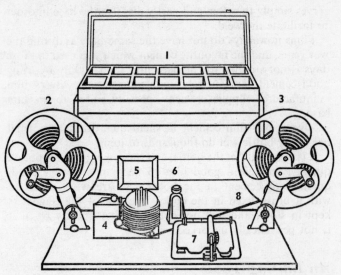

The editing table contains all the equipment for editing and splicing films. The individual takes are stored in the pigeon holes (1), and wound-up on to the reel (3). The animated viewer (4) projects the film on to the miniature screen (5) (p. 141). Other items include the splicer (7), and film cement (6). The take-up reel (2), holds the edited film as it grows in length.

Plastic spools are practically unbreakable, and better to handle than aluminium.

If you have a viewer, make a final check of the film on it, rather than on the projector. Run the film slowly. If there are any points needing attention, such as a bad frame to be cut out, mark it with a punch.

Don't project a film immediately after assembling it—the joins may come unstuck.

Take Care of Your Films

Keep your films in closed tins with a humidifier to prevent the film drying out in course of time. Instead of a humidifier, you can use a small piece of blotting-paper moistened with water, or half water, half glycerine.

In hot countries films will keep best in small air-tight metal cabinets. Instead of a humidifier, use a few pieces of moisture absorbing material. Cabinets of this type are most suitable for storing any films of especial value.

Several firms undertake the waxing of films, which keeps them in better condition and helps to prevent scratching.

From time to time films should be rewound for examination and to dissipate any excess of moisture. Always check the splices carefully before projecting—any that were badly made may fail in the projector.

If your projector is over-oiled the film will pick up oil and dirt. This, of course, should not happen with a properly designed projector, but on some machines the oil leaks out when they are running.

Clean your films with carbon tetrachloride which is an excellent grease solvent for all purposes.

The Projector

THE projector is a necessary complement of the camera. It reconstructs on the screen the pictures which you shot in your camera. On the choice of projector, and on its technical refinements, depend the final results.

The components of a projector can be divided into three groups: the light source, the mechanics, and the optical system. You should know the various features of these components to help you to choose your projector wisely.

The Light Source

The quality of the picture on the screen depends to a very large extent upon the amount of light available. But it is essential that the light should be used efficiently—that is the job of the optical components (p. 156).

Practically all manufacturers adopt a lamp of a power between 300 and 500 watts. A few machines still use a 200-watt lamp, but can nevertheless accommodate a more powerful lamp, say 300 watts. Machines intended for projection over a long throw are made to take lamps of 750, or exceptionally, 1,000 watts.

The bulb is usually tubular, with a black-painted cap at the top; this cap is most important, since it prevents light shining out of the top of the lamphouse, on to the projector and everything around. If the lamp has no black tip, it is possible to buy small metal caps specially made for the purpose.

The standard lamps used in amateur cine projectors have a so-called prefocus cap. This cap is cylindrical, with a centre contact and a locating flange in two parts, one larger than the other. The lampholder has two recesses to match, and the lamp is automatically centred when it is inserted.

It may occasionally happen that a lamp will not go into the holder, or is very stiff. In that case file off a little metal from the flanges to make the lamp fit into the holder.

Some lamps of the smaller sizes (200 or 300 watts) are made with a small bayonet cap, and a few old machines use Edison screw caps. It is advisable to change the latter holder for a prefocus type.

Current Supply

In some projectors the lamp is run off the mains voltage. In this case, you must simply make sure that the lamp is of the correct voltage for the mains—in Great Britain generally 220 to 240 volts, and in the United States and many European countries 110 to 115 volts.

The lower voltage lamp has a considerably higher light output and a longer life, and even where the mains are of the higher voltage it is generally preferred to use a 110 volt lamp. In this case, some means of reducing the voltage are necessary.

Sometimes the motor also runs on 110 volts, but on British machines more often at 200-250 volts.

There are two methods of reducing the mains voltage to the lamp voltage. The first is by means of a resistance. This is relatively inexpensive, but it is very wasteful of current, since the surplus voltage is simply dissipated as heat. It is, however, the only simple device suitable for D.C. mains.

For A.C. supplies which are now almost universal, a transformer is more efficient. Sometimes this is built into the projector, in others it forms a separate unit.

On the primary side—the windings connected to the mains—there will be several terminals for different voltages, from 200 to 250. The secondary—the windings connected to the lamp—will probably give only 110 volts, or occasionally 115 volts. The latter is useful when an extra bright picture is required, although of course it reduces the life of your lamp.

Low-voltage Lamps

On certain projectors the lamp works on a lower voltage, for instance 75 volts, instead of 110 volts. This type of lamp has more robust filaments, and consequently has a longer life and a higher light output.

Even better is a lamp of still lower voltage, for instance 24 volts. At this voltage a 400-volt lamp has a theoretical light output of 14,000 lumens, as against a lamp of the same wattage at 115 volts, which has an output of only 9,600 lumens. The life of the former lamp is 100 hours, while the 110 volt lamp has a life of only 25 hours.

The low-voltage lamp is especially advantageous for showing colour films. Because the filament burns at a higher temperature the light is whiter. It is still possible— for instance for a particularly dense film—to over-run the lamp occasionally to obtain just that bit more light.

The Lamp in Use

A switch is always provided to switch the lamp on and off. In some machines this switch is combined with a variable resistance controlling the lamp current, so that the switch operates only at a minimum current.

The life of lamps is increased if the current is not applied abruptly to the filaments. A pre-heating device feeds the lamp in two stages: first when the current is switched on the filament just glows red, and then comes to full brightness when the full current is switched on.

This effect may also be obtained by means of a variable resistance, or a tapped transformer with a two-way switch.

In the more expensive projectors an ammeter is built into the base, indicating the maximum current which should be exceeded only for brief periods.

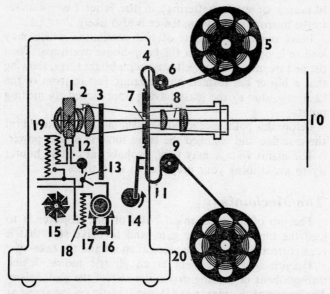

The essential parts of the projector are the optical system, motor and film transport. The light source comprises the lamp (1), with its pre-heating resistor (19), and adjustable resistor (18). It is cooled by the fan (15). A voltage dropping transformer can be connected across (12), (13) for low-voltage lamps. The condenser (2), concentrates the light on the gate (7), and the lens (8), projects the film image on to the screen (10). The motor (16), controlled from the switch (17), also operates the film transport (14) and the shutter (13). The film from the feed spool (5) passes round the roller (6), and forms a large loop (4), before entering the gate (7). After leaving the gate the film forms a second loop (11), and passes over the roller (9) to the take-up spool (20).

Make sure the lamp has a black cap, either painted on the lamp or attached to it; it prevents stray light from the top of the lamp-house.

Never use a larger lamp than the ventilating system allows for; if the machine seems to be over-heating, stop the projector and if possible let the fan run by itself for a while.

Insufficient cooling of the lamp may result in the bulb

blistering or even shattering; in the latter case, damage to the mirror and first condenser is also likely.

Look out for any signs of bad ventilation which may lead to lamp failure. First the lamp-house overheats. Then the picture may become yellowish with bright rings, showing that a blister has formed on the lamp, just in front of the filaments, due to the glass having approached its melting point.

Before this point is reached, you should have switched off the machine and changed the lamp for one of less power.

The mains voltage may vary, probably at certain hours; try to avoid using your projector at such times.

The Mechanism

The job of the mechanical parts of the projector is to feed the film through the gate, and to make sure that it runs correctly between the take-off spool and the take-up.

The principal component is an electric motor, which through belts or gearing drives the rest of the mechanism. The power of the motor will depend partly on the speed at which the machine is intended to run; a machine built to run at 24 frames a second will need a larger motor than one intended to run only at silent speed (16 frames).

Don't overload the motor by running faster than its normal speed, or by running spools larger than the machine is built for.

Generally 8 mm. projectors are made to carry 200 feet spools, giving over a quarter of an hour's running time. Even if the spool arms are long enough to carry 400 feet spools, it is not wise to use spools of this size unless the machine is designed to take them.

The Sprockets and Transport

There may be either one or two sprockets. Their job is to feed the film evenly from the take-off spool and back to the take-up.

152

The sprocket is a drum with teeth, on which the film is retained by shoes or sometimes by a roller either side of the sprocket.

When there is only a single sprocket in the centre, the films runs over the upper part of it forming the upper loop by means of a stripper plate. From the lower end of the gate the film runs to the under part of the sprocket.

The majority of projectors have a feed sprocket and a take-up sprocket. The two are identical, but work in opposite senses. Between the take-off sprocket and the gate there must be a fairly large loop, and again as the film leaves the gate there must be a second loop of about the same size, before the film engages with the lower sprocket.

With one exception, the film is always fed through the gate itself by means of a claw motion. There are two or three claws mounted at the right-hand side of the gate.

The reason for using two or three claws is that the strain of feeding the film is distributed over several perforations, and film damage is less likely to occur. If the film should have a damaged perforation it will still run through the projector.

The film is held flat in the gate by means of a pressure plate. Each frame stops for a fraction of a second behind the projection aperture, then the claws engage the perforations and bring the next frame into position, and so on, at a minimum speed of 16 frames per second.

The Shutter

The shutter cannot be seen from the outside of the projector, and it is usually necessary to remove other parts to get at it.

It consists of a disc with sectors cut out. When a shutter blade is in the light beam it intercepts the light, and when a cut-out sector passes the beam, light is allowed to pass and form an image on the screen.

One of the shutter blades serves to mask the movement of the film in the gate.

The flicker sometimes seen on the screen when the projector runs slowly shows that the light cut-off must occur at a certain minimum rate, otherwise persistence of vision does not come into play to produce a continuous image. Actually the majority of projector shutters are arranged to cut the light 32 times a second when the projector is running at 16 frames.

In some projectors the shutter is either interchangeable or adjustable. Manufacturers sometimes recommend a two-bladed shutter when projecting at a long throw, while for a smaller room a three-bladed shutter gives better results.

Sometimes the change from one to the other, instead of necessitating a change of the shutter, is effected by shifting one of the blades.

This point may be important. With a three-bladed shutter, for instance, it is possible to reduce the film speed to 12 frames a second without getting flicker. Naturally there will be some loss of light, but it will not be serious on a small screen.

Often it is quite useful to have a projector which will run without flicker at a lower speed than normal. Cameras do not always run at exactly 16 frames—chargers have a tendency to slow down the film.

The Path of the Film

The film runs from the feed spool over the sprocket, through the gate, and back over the sprocket on to the take-up spool.

At the top and bottom of the gate the film must form loops. The loops have to be large enough for the film to run freely, but naturally you must take care that the film does not rub on any part of the machine.

There is a tendency at times for the lower loop to disappear. To avoid any risk of film damage, there is on some of the more expensive machines an automatic device which maintains the loop.

In the gate some projectors have a framing or racking device. Its purpose is to centre the picture in the projection aperture. This is done in some machines by sliding the gate or the aperture plate, while in others it is the lens that moves.

When there is only a single sprocket the film returns to the spool round the lower face of the sprocket. If there is a separate take-up sprocket, the film is held against it by a shoe or rollers.

The position of the feed and take-up spools is unimportant, but the film should be wound *emulsion out*, with the perforations on the right when the feed spool is in position on the projector.

It is logical that the take-up spool should also wind the film emulsion out, although this may mean crossing the belt.

The take-up spool is driven by the motor through a belt, or on the more costly machines through gearing.

To avoid strain on the film, it is wise when running to remove the belt from the take-off spool.

Points of the Motor

When you switch on, the switch first starts the motor. A resistance varies the speed; always run quite slowly at the beginning to check your threading. Have a long film lead so that you do not reach the pictures too soon.

A second switch lights the lamp, the filaments of which will already be red-hot if the machine has a pre-heating circuit.

Not all machines have a reversing drive; this does not affect the running of the projector. The motor is reversed by a third switch.

If you use the projector reverse as a trick effect, don't overdo it. The real use of the reverse is to run the same scene several times, and in this case the light should be masked when the film is running backwards.

Most projectors have a motor rewind which serves a double purpose. Besides winding the film back rapidly to the take-off spool, at the end of the show, it cools down the lamp. Again, always rewind emulsion out.

If the motor tends to overheat it is wise to rewind by hand. There is in any case much to recommend this practice; you have the chance of checking your joins and cleaning or dusting the film.

Dual Gauge Projectors

There are a number of projectors on which you can run either of the two larger gauges of film, 16 mm. and 9.5 mm. But the adaptation of a projector to run either of these gauges as well as 8 mm. leads generally to some inefficiency, because of the much smaller picture of the 8 mm. film.

However, such a dual-gauge machine may be very useful if you or your friends have films in both gauges. There are several ways of dual operation.

Some models have a complete double track, and the change from one gauge to the other takes a matter of seconds. Other types are made in a triple-gauge form, running equally 16 mm., 9.5 mm., or 8 mm.; in this case the whole of the film path is rapidly interchanged.

The Optical System

As an indication of the importance of the optical components, a projector with a lamp of only 300 watts but with an efficient optical system may give as bright a picture as another machine with a 500 watt lamp.

The optical system of a projector starts with the mirror behind the lamp. Its job is to reflect the light from the lamp back to the condenser.

The mirror is generally adjustable for height, but sometimes it is fixed, and forms part of the lamp-house. In that

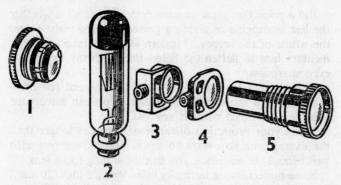

The optical system of the projector consists of the mirror (1) which reflects the light from the lamp (2) through the condensers (3), (4) on to the film (not shown). The lens (5) then projects the image.

case the lamp is adjustable in order to centre the filaments correctly.

The condenser consists of two or three lenses, and sometimes a heat-absorbing glass in two sections. The condenser serves to concentrate the light from the lamp upon the film in the projector aperture. Its job is not always efficiently done—this is the main difference, from the point of view of light output, between a good projector and others.

In 8 mm. projectors, the luminous surface of the lamp is larger than the area of the film frame, so the condenser must work at maximum efficiency to avoid loss of light.

As with all lenses, periodical cleaning is necessary. It is unfortunate that in so many projectors it is by no means easy to dismantle the condenser.

The Projection Lens

Like the camera lens, it is available in different focal lengths and apertures. For 8 mm. film a normal focus is 1 inch or 25 mm.—double the focal length of the camera lens. The aperture ranges from $f\,2$ to $f\,1.5$.

But a point that must be considered first of all is whether the lens is capable of giving a perfectly sharp picture over the whole of the screen. Modern lenses include a supplementary lens to flatten the field—that is to say to achieve even sharpness.

A projection lens should always be bloomed (p. 19)— it results in a more brilliant image. You can have your older lens bloomed without any risk.

When your projection distance or throw is longer than the average, or you want to avoid putting the projector well behind the audience, you can use a long-focus lens.

Some projectors are normally fitted with a ¾ inch (20 mm.) lens instead of the usual 1 inch one. This slight difference in focal length means that the picture on the screen will be larger, or for a given size of picture the throw will be shorter. It may be useful if you have to give a show in a small room.

An afocal attachment may be used to increase the size of the picture during the programme. This is just a trick effect unlikely to be seen in the cinema; it is produced simply by fitting a supplementary lens to the projector.

A blue filter is a further projection accessory. Some people find a bluish picture more pleasing and more restful for the eyes.

SIZE OF PICTURE ON PROJECTION

Throw (Feet)	¾ Inch (19 mm.)	1 Inch (25 mm.)	1¼ Inches (32 mm.)	1½ Inches (38 mm.)	2 Inches (50 mm.)
3	0/8 ×0/6	—	—	—	—
5	1/1½×0/10	0/10×0/7½	0/8 ×0/6	—	—
7	1/7 ×1/2½	1/2 ×0/10½	0/11½×0/9	0/9½×0/7	—
10	2/3 ×1/9	1/9 ×1/4	1/4 ×1/10	1/11½×0/10½	0/10×0/7½
15	3/5 ×2/7	2/6 ×1/11	2/0 ×1/6	1/8 ×1/3	1/3 ×0/11½
20	4/6 ×3/6	3/5 ×2/7	2/9× ×2/1	2/3 ×1/9	1/8 ×1/3
25	5/8 ×4/4	4/3 ×3/3	3/5 ×2/8	2/10×2/2	2/2 ×1/8
50	—	8/6 ×6/6	6/9 ×5/3	5/8 ×4/4	4/3 ×3/3

Maintenance

Get to know all the parts of your projector, so that you will not fumble about before an impatient audience.

The working parts have quite a hard job; oil them as necessary. The oiling points are generally marked in red, or sometimes they have oiling cups.

Always use the grade of oil recommended by the manufacturers. Too thin an oil will not lubricate adequately, a too thick oil may cause accidents in winter.

Oil your projector before every show, and periodically when it is not in use.

The condition of your films depends on the state of the gate. The gate must be perfectly clean, for dirt may come off the film during projection. The gate and aperture must be cleaned after every reel, otherwise the edges of the picture will not be clean on the screen.

Sometimes the gate may cause film scratching. Don't attempt to re-polish it—get a new part. This detail is of prime importance, and you should bear it in mind when buying a projector.

Never clean the gate with anything metal. Use a quill, a small brush or a match-stick.

If you find oil collects on the base of your machine, wipe it after every show. Oil is frequently a cause of electrical breakdowns, rotting the insulation and causing shorts.

Choosing a Projector

In choosing a projector, take the following points into consideration.

Your films are valuable and you must be able to project them often without premature deterioration.

The gate and pressure plate are the principal causes of scratching. Here the finish and smoothness are most important.

If your projector overheats it will quickly ruin not only the lamp, but your films, which will get dry and brittle. So see that the lamp and gate are adequately cooled.

The quality of your picture depends upon the light source and optical system. The lamp should give enough light for a picture at least 3 feet wide. Its light must be efficiently used, and not wasted. The lens must produce a perfectly sharp picture, without loss of focus around the edges.

A projector is not just a costly toy, but a piece of apparatus which you will be proud to show to your friends. It must be simple to handle and not so noisy that you have to instal it in another room. The noise of a modern projector should not spoil the musical accompaniment which you will arrange for each programme.

A point that should not be overlooked is whether you can subsequently change your projector for something more up-to-date. Progress never stops, and every year improved equipment appears. A machine of known make and high quality can be more easily exchanged for a later model.

The Screen

You can project your picture on a white wall or a white-washed sheet, but you will get a much better picture if you use a proper screen.

It is just as important to choose the right screen as the right projector. To a large extent picture quality depends on your screen.

It is better with 8 mm. film to be satisfied with a 3 feet picture, even if your projector will give a larger picture.

The main difference between various screen surfaces is the way in which they reflect light.

We say a screen is directional if it reflects most of the light in one direction. To people viewing the screen from that direction the screen appears brighter, while people sitting in other positions see a dimmer picture.

The white matt screen should rarely be used for shows at home. It has no directional properties and reflects back to the audience only a small proportion of the light. It

The choice of screen surface depends on the angle at which it has to be viewed. A beaded screen will give the most brilliant image, but is restricted to a narrow angle (**4**). For a wider angle (**3**), a silvered screen is better, though not as brilliant in the centre as a beaded one. A matt white screen is less efficient still, but less directional and thus that is usable over a very wide area (**1**) and (**2**).

may be useful if you have a powerful projector and a large audience.

Metallised screens give satisfactory results at moderate prices. Their reflecting power is fair, and the directional property is no trouble for home shows. The surface must be smooth and evenly painted—a single layer of aluminium paint does not make a good screen.

The beaded screen, in spite of its strongly directional properties, is still the best type of screen. You will get the best possible results with a good beaded screen and a fairly powerful projector.

The beads must cover the screen surface evenly, and must

Portable wall screens (*right*) are simply suspended from the wall and roll up. The same type of screen can also be suspended from a tripod stand (*left*).

be very small, otherwise the image will look grainy. Your audience should sit as close as possible to the centre line of the screen, since the brightness of the picture falls off quickly for people sitting off-centre.

The beaded screen has the unusual property of reflecting the bulk of the light back towards the projector, almost regardless of the angle of the screen. It is efficient only if your projector is central with the audience.

A glass screen gives a brilliant grain-free picture. Like all good reflecting surfaces it is strongly directional.

Your picture will always look better if you frame it with a black mask to suit the size of the picture. The masking will set limits to the size of the picture and will prevent dust in the aperture showing round the edges of the picture.

Screen Supports

Some screens, particularly matt and metallised types, are supplied on a wood roller. A second roller at the bottom

162

of the screen keeps it flat. This simple arrangement is inexpensive, but it is not easy to roll up a metal screen without creasing and spoiling it.

A better idea is the use of side struts for tensioning the screen, the whole arrangement being fixed to the wall or mounted on a tripod. The screen is wound and unwound by hand.

Some screens are enclosed in a cylindrical case, and a spring keeps the screen taut and rolls it up again after the show.

The case is mounted on a tripod with an extension rod; the top of the screen is hooked on to this rod, while the cylinder keeps the screen rigid and flat.

Other screens are built into a carrying case, and a spring device rolls up the screen after the show. The box is weighted, and can be placed on a piece of furniture. This is possibly the quickest and simplest arrangement for fitting up the screen and packing it for transport. It is at the same time as versatile as any hanging screen.

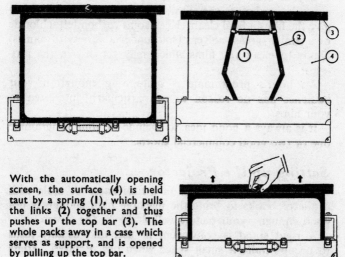

With the automatically opening screen, the surface (4) is held taut by a spring (1), which pulls the links (2) together and thus pushes up the top bar (3). The whole packs away in a case which serves as support, and is opened by pulling up the top bar.

Presenting the Show

YOUR private cinema shows should be regarded as a treat—but they won't be unless you have everything prepared in advance.

Making up the Programme

Don't give way to the impatience of your family and show your films before you have viewed them, cut and edited them.

Even if you have no time to edit them properly, and to arrange the scenes in logical order or according to plan, at least cut out any bad shots and join the rolls of film together on one or more large spools.

If your films are already edited, it is wise to view them a few hours before the show, to check all the splices and give the films a final clean. Keep some carbon tetrachloride or a similar grease-solvent (sold under a variety of names) handy to clean any films which may get oily in the projector.

An hour's programme is quite long enough if your audience has no reason to be particularly interested in your films.

It is always a good idea to include in your programme one or two good commercial shorts.

Setting up the Projector

Your projector must be on a firm base. A table with a pile of books to bring the machine high enough is not good enough—your picture will shake on the screen.

A rigid stand is convenient in use, and usually folds to occupy quite a small space when not required. Some

164

The ideal home projection arrangement is to have the screen in a bay window and project along the length of the room (*left*). If that is impossible, project obliquely to increase the throw (*right*); but watch out for image distortion.

models have shelves for spools and possibly for a record-player.

A stand with castors makes for ease in positioning the projector, while jacks keep it firm once it is in the right place.

Your projector should always be in good working order. Run it for a few moments before threading up. Always clean the gate, the optical system and the aperture before threading.

Put a long leader at the start of the film. While it is running through you will be able to make sure the projector is working properly before you switch on the lamp.

Check the condition of your take-up spool. Keep it in a metal can, and not just slipped into the projector case.

Make sure you have just the right amount of oil in the machine. Too much oil will make your films oily, and on some machines spread over the back of the lens.

Always have handy a spare lamp, spare motor and take-up belts, fuses or fuse wire, a torch, and a screw-driver.

If your projector is noisy, put it on a rubber mat, or

better still, in the next room, showing through the half-open door.

Your film may break or a splice come undone while you are showing. A piece of adhesive cellophane tape will make a temporary join.

Preparing the Auditorium

Set your screen at a reasonable distance from the projector, according to the power of the lamp. A small well-lit picture is better than a large one which in any case will look out of focus to people in the front row.

If for any reason you cannot position your projector in advance, get everything ready so that you do not waste time on preparations.

For good results your projector must be upright, and the axis perpendicular to the screen.

Unless your projector has a pilot lamp, keep a small lamp burning near the projector, but shaded from the audience.

Running the Show

In the projector the film should always have its emulsion (the matt side) facing the screen, with the perforations to the right to match the position of sprocket teeth and claws. The pictures on the film must be upside down in the gate.

Never wind too much film on your spools, or it may come unwound while you are threading. It is possible to buy clips which grip the cheeks of the spool and secure the film.

Before your audience arrives, make sure the picture is properly centred on the screen, and that it is in focus and in rack.

When everything is ready, gradually dim the room lighting.

Make sure the projector lamp has a black cap on it (p. 148) otherwise you will find at this stage there is a blaze of light around the projector, which will ruin the picture.

You can arrange a musical accompaniment which may be interrupted by your commentary.

At the end of the reel, switch on your pilot lamp and one of the room lights, but not all the lamps, otherwise the audience will be dazzled.

Don't rewind right away—get on with the show. Change the feed spool over to take-up.

Keep your performance fairly short—don't strain the patience of your guests.

If your programme includes black-and-white and colour films, always run the colour last. The lamp must run at its full marked voltage, otherwise the picture will look too yellow and other colours will not be true either.

Musical Accompaniment

Always arrange a musical accompaniment, even if it has little to do with your films. It will mask the noise of the projector. You can easily arrange for music by means of records, and a record player.

The ordinary record player consists of an electric motor, a fairly heavy turn-table acting as a flywheel, an automatic stop device, and speed adjustment. You can check the running speed by means of a stroboscope—either markings around the edge of the turn-table, or a cardboard disc slipped on to the centre pin. It is important that the speed should be perfectly uniform, particularly if you are using a double turn-table—any change in speed alters the pitch of the music.

The pick-up is connected either to its own amplifier, or more simply to the special socket on your radio set. The volume control will permit you to adjust the loudness of the sound, and a tone control is desirable.

Double Turn-tables

A double turn-table with two pick-ups will enable you to run an uninterrupted musical accompaniment.

Choose a good quality motor, free from noise and vibration, with a 12-inch turn-table. The ordinary gramo-

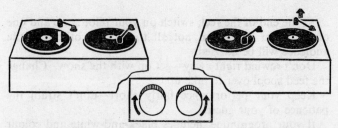

To change over from one record to another on a double turn-table, lower the second pick-up on to the record, as the first record nears its end (*left*). Mix from the first to the second by means of the volume control (*centre*), and then lift off the first pick-up (*right*).

phone motor will run at different speeds, but can be set to run fairly constantly at 78 r.p.m.

For the modern micro-groove records, motors are made with three speeds, $33\frac{1}{3}$, 45 and 78 r.p.m. There is no need for two motors with variable speeds; one can be an ordinary single-speed motor and the other a three-speed one.

Choose the latter motor very carefully. The turn-table must be free from vibration while running, and the $33\frac{1}{3}$ and 45 r.p.m. speeds must be constant. The table must be perfectly level.

An automatic record-changer is not necessary, and may even hinder you in changing the discs and switching from one to another.

Any radio mechanic can undertake the construction of a double turn-table, which should have the following features.

The two motors and pick-ups must be on the same base-board, the pick-ups to the right of the turn-tables. A three-way switch will enable you to use either the right-hand or the left-hand pick-up, or both together.

Each pick-up must have its own volume control. A tone control should complete the equipment.

The output from the pick-ups is taken to the appropriate socket of your radio set. Naturally a separate amplifier is better, but is not essential.

168

If you are using long-playing discs, make sure you have sufficient amplification. You may have to add another valve to obtain enough volume.

Choice of Discs

Choose for preference light music which your audience can follow easily, and which as far as possible matches the films. You can buy discs of effects and noises of all sorts.

Don't use records of songs; the words may distract the attention of your audience from the film.

Don't try to ape the professional; keep your amateur status, but put over your films pleasingly.

Tape Recorders

Instead of the gramophone, you can also use a tape-recorder to provide the music. This has the advantage that you can record the sound yourself—e.g., from the wireless, and mix it with a spoken commentary.

The tape-recorder is even easier to use than a gramophone, for there is no changing-over required during the show. One reel of tape can play up to an hour's programme.

Some tape-recorders incorporate their own amplifier, or you can use a recorder deck only (i.e., the recording and playing heads together with the motor and reels) and join it to a radio set.

You can further erase any recording whenever you want to, and immediately record a fresh one on the same tape.

The operational parts of a typical tape-recorder are the volume control (1), the motor control (2), the tone control (3), sound head (4), the tape spools (5), (6), and the tape itself (7). A microphone is usually provided.

Magnetic Sound

MODERN magnetic recording technique puts at your disposal a simple and economical means of adding sound to all your films, old or new, shot at the silent speed of 16 frames per second.

Commercially produced silent films can have sound added to them just as simply. The recording never wears out, it can be erased, altered, re-recorded just as you like. The sound can be played back immediately it is recorded, and as many times as you like.

Magnetic sound for 8 mm. is comparatively new—it has only just become available to the amateur. In years to come still further improvements may come about. But right now you can look out all your old films and give them speech and music. Your film shows will no longer be silent, but, with magnetic recording, will have sound correctly matched to the picture.

There are four essentials to make your films speak:

1. Recording material.
2. Erasing, recording and reproducing apparatus.
3. Mechanical means for feeding the film.
4. Electronic components—the amplifier and its acoustic complements, the microphone, turn-tables, pick-ups.

The Recording Material

Commercial magnetic sound recording systems use as their recording medium either a soft steel wire, or an acetate tape coated with magnetic material.

But for 8 mm. films the solution is still simpler.

First your film must be completely edited and titled,

with the splices well made and carefully checked. You then send your film to a suitable firm which "stripes" it— i.e., coats a narrow strip of magnetic material along its whole length.

Two methods of striping have been proposed.

In the first, the magnetic stripe is coated between the perforations and the edge of the film; unfortunately the nearness of the perforations tends to introduce an unwanted noise clearly audible in the loudspeaker.

In the second method, this difficulty is overcome but a mechanical difficulty is introduced: the striping is coated on the other edge of the film.

In whichever position the film is striped, it is always coated on the base or glossy side of the film, except in the case of duplicate prints—either black-and-white or Koda-chrome. These have the emulsion on the opposite side from usual, and the striping has to be coated over the emulsion. Although this may be less satisfactory, it does not seem to cause any difficulty.

The film so treated is ready to record sound. The special quality coating enables sound to be recorded at the low film speed of $2\frac{2}{5}$ inches per second—the running speed of 8 mm. films at the normal rate of 16 frames per second.

Erasing, Recording and Reproducing

These three functions are provided on the one outfit. Sometimes they are effected by a single magnet head serving all three purposes or by two heads, the first acting as eraser and the other for recording and reproduction.

The erasing head is always placed before the recording head. As its name suggests, it erases everything previously recorded on the magnetic strips before a new recording is made.

In recorders with only a single magnet head, the film must be erased before it is recorded.

The recording head comes next. It is connected to the

171

amplifier, into which sound is fed either from a microphone or a pick-up, or from a radio. The amplifier transfers the modulations to the magnetic stripe on the film.

The reproducing head reproduces the sounds recorded a few seconds earlier, by means of the same amplifier and a speaker.

The Film Feed

As it comes out of the projector gate the film passes over the magnet heads. According to the design of the machine, there may be one or two heads serving the three purposes of erasing, recording and reproducing. A flywheel keeps the film moving at constant speed.

The projector motor may not be powerful enough to drive the film transport both in the gate and on the sound head, and may have to be replaced. It must run at a perfectly uniform speed of 16 frames per second, both for recording, and for projection and reproduction.

The Amplifier

You should have a good amplifier of average power (say 5 watts undistorted output). The amplifier must be at least equivalent in quality to that of the modern record player. It amplifies the sound both in recording and reproduction. It should incorporate a volume control with a "magic eye" or neon indicator, and mixing controls.

If you have been accompanying your films with sound

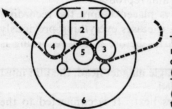

The sound head consists of the magnetic head (2), itself mounted on the base plate (1), the rollers (3), (4), and the sound drum (5). This is connected to the flywheel (6) to ensure constant speed of travel of the film (dotted).

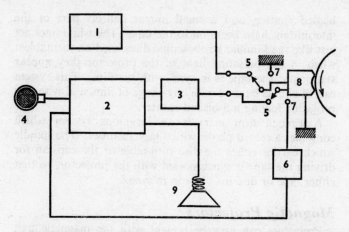

In this scheme of a magnetic sound unit, the recording section consists of a high-frequency oscillator (1), the amplifier (2), into which the output of the microphone (4) is fed, and the recording equaliser (3). The reproduction section again uses the amplifier (2), together with a reproduction equaliser (6); the output goes into the loudspeaker (9). The sound head (8) can be connected either to the recording circuit—positions (5), (5)—or to the reproducing circuit—positions (7), (7).

from a record player, you will probably have most of this equipment. You then merely add the recording equipment to your projector.

Synchronising Magnetic Sound

The better tape recorders run at a sufficiently constant speed to maintain synchronism between the film and a recorded commentary, provided the tape is recorded and reproduced on the same apparatus. There are several methods of ensuring closer synchronism; for instance, the projector and recorder may be driven by synchronous motors.

In an ingenious system of American origin, so-called "tiger" tape is used; on the back of this tape are printed white lines, 15 to the inch. The projector must have a three-bladed shutter, and a small mirror deflects part of the intermittent light beam on to the tape. The white lines act just like the familiar stroboscopic discs used on turntables: when in the pulsating light of the projector they appear stationary, the tape is in sync. with the film. This system can of course be used with any gauge of film, and with any projector having a 3-bladed shutter.

A French firm markets an ingenious system which combines a record player with a tape recorder. The spindle which carries either the disc turn-table or the capstan for driving the tape is synchronised with the projector, so that either tape or disc may be run in sync.

Magnetic Projectors

Projectors can now be bought with the magnetic unit already fitted.

One projector, made in America, carries 1,600 feet of film—enough for a two-hour show. It is fitted with a 750 watt lamp, and can be run at either 16 or 24 frames per second (the latter naturally gives better sound quality). Sound can be recorded from either a microphone or disc, which may be used simultaneously in order to provide music to a commentary.

But it is quite simple to adapt any projector. You will need the pre-amplifier with "magic eye" control, but this is sometimes included with the record player.

How to Record

The job of recording is more easily done than described.

First send your edited film to a laboratory for striping. You must, of course, specify in which position the film is to be striped, for this has not yet been standardised. The film must be clean, and *not waxed*.

When your film is returned it is ready for recording.

Thread the film through the projector and over the recording head. Always allow a long leader to the film, and let the projector warm up before starting recording, so that it will quickly come up to speed.

Always make sure the magnetic stripe is completely erased by running the film through the erasing head before recording.

If there is a separate erasing head mounted in advance of the recording head, keep the erasing head switched on all the time you are recording. In equipment with a single head the film must be run through for erasing and again for recording.

With the film correctly threaded for recording, project the picture and either run your record player or speak into the microphone, or both at once. The potentiometer in the pre-amplifier enables you to adjust the volume for each channel, while the "magic eye" (either the single or double type) gives a visual control of the volume being recorded.

If you make a mistake or "fluff" your lines, just run back until you come to a pause and start again from that point.

When you have finished recording, rewind your film, run it through the projector with the reproducer head in circuit, and the loud-speaker connected to the amplifier output. If the erasing head is separate from the recording-reproducing head, make sure it is switched off, otherwise all your recording will be accidentally erased.

In most types of equipment the same head serves the two purposes of recording and reproduction. Naturally the internal circuits are changed over, but this does not concern you. Just turn a knob and you change from recording to reproduction, and the speaker reproduces everything you have just recorded, in perfect synchronism with the picture.

That is all there is to magnetic recording on cine film.

You will soon be able to do the job in recording studios. Your dealer will undertake the striping of your film and provide facilities for recording, putting at your disposal record players, microphone and visual control on the pre-amplifier. You then take home a recorded film, ready to run through your own magnetic sound projector.

Indexed Glossary

176

177

Some items of equipment or certain materials mentioned in this book may not be freely available in every country. Import and marketing conditions vary widely, and are beyond the control of the photographic retailer.

FOCAL BOOKS ON PHOTOGRAPHY

PHOTO TECHNIQUE
By H. J. Walls, B.Sc., Ph.D.
Designed as a reasoned introduction to the fundamentals of practical camera work: a thinking person's guide to sound photography.
384 pp., 305 illus. **Price 25/-**

DEVELOPING
By C. I. Jacobson, Ph.D.
Practical advice on negative technique, choosing the right chemicals and getting the right negative, passed on in straightforward language.
328 pp., 150 illus., 13th ed. **Price 17/6**

PHOTOGRAPHIC OPTICS
By Arthur Cox, M.A., B.Sc., F.Inst.P.
Every photographer should be able to discriminate between lenses just as he knows how to choose films or filters. It pays to know how they work and how to work with them.
376 pp., 352 illus., 11th ed. **Price 17/6**

EXPOSURE
By W. F. Berg, D.Sc., Ph.D., F.R.P.S.
Helps to pick the right tools and materials, to suit filters to film and subject, to determine the correct exposure.
448 pp., 201 illus., 2nd ed. **Price 21/-**

LIGHTING FOR PHOTOGRAPHY
By W. Nurnberg, F.R.P.S., F.I.B.P.
The technical roots of artificial lighting, the advantages and limitations of different light sources, the principles of their practical use.
176 pp., 285 illus., 13th ed. **Price 21/-**

PHOTO-FLASH IN PRACTICE
By Geoffrey Gilbert
Extensively revised and brought up-to-date. Contains plans for making mains or battery electronic flash units, battery capacitor flashgun, magnetic synchronizer.
304 pp., 163 illus., 4th ed. **Price 17/6**

MAKING LANTERN SLIDES AND FILMSTRIPS
By C. Douglas Milner
This book sorts out the best from traditional experience and combines it with the results of modern research.
224 pp., 85 illus., 2nd ed. **Price 12/6**

COMPLETE ART OF PRINTING AND ENLARGING
By O. R. Croy, Ph.D.
How to make prints—ordinary prints, elaborately controlled or very tricky prints; a wealth of technical knowledge and personal experience.
256 pp., 443 illus., 5th ed. **Price 21/-**

ENLARGING
By C. I. Jacobson, Ph.D.
The photographer's ability to judge negatives, apparatus, paper and chemicals, is turned into terms of practical experience in this book.
312 pp., 130 illus., 16th ed. **Price 17/6**

SENSITOMETRY
By L. Lobel and M. Dubois
Explains the basic facts which any photographer needs to know about emulsions and their properties, and covers apparatus and methods used.
264 pp., 102 illus. **Price 25/-**

RETOUCHING
By O. R. Croy, Ph.D.
This book points out the ways, picks the tools, explains the best methods and shows correct examples.
200 pp., 304 illus. **Price 17/6**

LIGHTING FOR PORTRAITURE
By W. Nurnberg, F.R.P.S., F.I.B.P.
With extreme clarity and profuse illustrations, the author of *Lighting for Photography* here describes the manifold possibilities of lighting the human face.
192 pp., 509 illus., 2nd ed. **Price 17/6**

PHOTOGRAPHIC ILLUMINATION
By R. Howard Cricks, F.R.P.S., F.B.K.S.
Tells all the photographer needs to know about electrical theory, the latest equipment and how to get the most out of it.
320 pp., 90 illus. **Price 17/6**

FILMSTRIP AND SLIDE PROJECTION
By M. K. Kidd and C. W. Long
How to choose your projector, set it up and handle its electrical factors; fit up projection rooms; make a projector.
160 pp., 62 illus. **Price 7/6**

FOCAL BOOKS ON PHOTOGRAPHY

ALL THE PHOTO TRICKS
By Edwin Smith
Shows how startling pictorial effects, fantastic variations of reality, amusing deceptions of the eye and even political propaganda are worked through photography.
280 pp., 157 illus., 6th ed.   **Price 17/6**

COLOUR BOOK OF PHOTOGRAPHY
By Lucien Lorelle
A full account of colour photography on a down-to-earth, practical level—in terms of pictures rather than processes—abounding in advice, facts, hints.
212 pp., 132 illus., 2nd ed.   **Price 12/6**

T.V. IN THE MAKING
Edited by Paul Rotha
A comprehensive survey of the many fields opening up in the expanding world of television. Each aspect is covered by an authority on his subject.
216 pp.   **Price 25/-**

A PHOTOGRAPHIC PILGRIM'S PROGRESS
By Charles Duncan
Mellowed experience, kindly humour and pointed advice from a veteran of photography to warm the heart of the old and encourage the young.
160 pp.   **Price 12/6**

35 mm. PHOTO TECHNIQUE
By H. S. Newcombe, F.R.P.S.
Technical factors of film, exposure and development producing the perfect negative are put into the language of common-sense for the practical man.
320 pp., 148 illus., 11th ed.   **Price 19/6**

THE LEICA WAY
By Andrew Matheson
Covers the technique and art of Leica photography both with the latest equipment and older models and accessories.
426 pp., 354 illus., 3rd ed.   **Price 21/-**

THE CONTAX WAY
By H. Freytag
Up-to-date facts and authoritative advice on all Contax equipment applied to every conceivable Contax subject.
280 pp., 286 illus., 5th ed.   **Price 21/-**

ALL-IN-ONE CAMERA BOOK
By W. D. Emanuel
The easy path to good photography is shown as a pleasant hobby with a technical background—the problems are simplified but not concealed.
232 pp., 116 illus., 38th ed.   **Price 10/6**

COLOUR PRINTS
By Jack H. Coote, F.R.P.S.
Goes into the methods of making colour prints, covering negative-positive processes, as well as the more traditional procedures for producing good colour prints.
328 pp., 40 illus.   **Price 25/-**

THE TECHNIQUE OF FILM EDITING
Compiled by Karel Reisz
Ten outstanding film editors summarize their views and experience and present the first comprehensive guide to their craft.
288 pp., 206 illus., 5th ed.   **Price 30/-**

MY WAY WITH THE MINIATURE
By Lancelot Vining, F.R.P.S., F.I.B.P.
Ten years more experience has gone into the thorough revision, ample additions and new illustrations of the present re-issue of this work.
260 pp., 109 illus., 11th ed.   **Price 15/6**

TWIN-LENS REFLEX COMPANION
By H. S. Newcombe, F.R.P.S.
Contributions on their twin-lens technique by ten American professional photographers of world-wide fame complement advice to beginner and advanced worker.
320 pp., 160 illus., 3rd ed.   **Price 17/6**

THE ROLLEI WAY
By L. A. Mannheim
A composite work, built from the experience and advice of leading photographers, dealing with essential points of Rolleiflex or Rolleicord practice.
232 pp., 278 illus., 5th ed.   **Price 17/6**

THE RETINA WAY
By O. R. Croy, Ph.D.
Will put the Retina technique safely in your hands and bring all the subjects of Retina photography within your reach.
304 pp., 228 illus., 7th ed.   **Price 21/-**

FOCAL BOOKS ON PHOTOGRAPHY

FOCAL CHARTS

FOCAL DEVELOPING CHART
By W. D. Emanuel

The right developing time at any temperature for your film and developer, fresh or used.

FOCAL EXPOSURE CHART
By W. D. Emanuel

Anywhere, any time, any subject, any light, any camera, any film.

FOCAL FILTER CHART
By W. D. Emanuel

The right filter, the right film, the right light, the right stop, the right speed for the right subject.

FOCAL FOCUSING CHART
By Arthur Cox

Sharp focus, safe depth, with any lens or attachment.

FOCAL LIGHTING CHART
By W. D. Emanuel

Simple lighting schemes, tested lamp positions, exact exposure values.

FOCAL STOP & SPEED CHART
By E. Steffens

A whole library of facts on exposure, depth and action.

FOCAL FLASH CHART
By W. D. Emanuel

Flash exposure disc, sun-flash exposure disc, ten typical set-ups.

FOCAL CINE CHART
By W. D. Emanuel

All the technical data needed.

Price 3/6 each (Postage 4d.)

FOCAL ENLARGING CHART
By W. D. Emanuel

Measures exposure, ensures sharpness, defines magnification.

Price 7/6 (Postage 9d.

CAMERA GUIDES

G.B.-B&H 624 GUIDE
MINOX GUIDE
BOLEX GUIDE
SPORTSTER GUIDE
BOLEX 8 mm. GUIDE
MOVIKON GUIDE
Price 7/6 each (Postage 9d.)

LEICA GUIDE
ROLLEIFLEX GUIDE
EXAKTA GUIDE
EXAKTA 35 mm. GUIDE
CONTAX GUIDE
WRAYFLEX GUIDE
CONTAFLEX GUIDE
RETINA GUIDE
PERIFLEX GUIDE
MICROCORD GUIDE
CONTINA GUIDE
Price 6/6 each (Postage 4d.)

ROBOT GUIDE
SUPER IKONTA GUIDE
Price 5/6 each (Postage 4d.)

PAXETTE GUIDE
KORELLE GUIDE
SELFIX GUIDE
PURMA GUIDE
KARAT GUIDE
VITESSA GUIDE
ISOLETTE GUIDE
NETTAR GUIDE
SILETTE GUIDE
BESSA-PERKEO GUIDE
VITO B GUIDE
ILOCA GUIDE
FUL-VUE GUIDE
COLORSNAP GUIDE
Price 4/6 each (Postage 4d.)

THE *focal* PHOTO GUIDES

The Most Popular Photographic Library in the World: 2/- each

PHOTOGUIDE MAGAZINE

the best

monthly

If you like the Photo Guides you will like the PhotoGuide Magazine even more. It is more lively and interesting than anything you have seen before.

Packed with the world's best photographs, drawings that make their point clear and a wide choice of reading matter.

You will find what you want; information and advice, experience and entertainment. All of it useful and never boring.

Photography is meant to be fun. The PhotoGuide Magazine is fun. It will help you to get more fun out of your camera—whatever camera you have.

The PhotoGuide Magazine keeps its feet firmly planted on the ground and yet it will fire your imagination. It will train your eye to find better pictures and help to improve your technique in getting them.

The PhotoGuide Magazine is worth every penny you pay for it and a lot more.

Is. 6d.

Subscription for a whole year **20s.** post free.

Send 2½d. stamp for free specimen copy.

PUBLISHED BY   FOCAL PRESS
31, FITZROY SQ.   LONDON, W.I

The Focal

ENCYCLOPEDIA

of

PHOTOGRAPHY

2,000 articles: 1¼ million words
1,468 pages, 385 photographs, 1,500 diagrams

Bound burgundy buckram, stamped gold

Price £5 5s.

THE FOCAL ENCYCLOPEDIA will do the job of a whole library. This single volume holds the right answers to any question on photography—ready for prompt reference. It contains more information than many books put together. Much of it could not easily be found elsewhere. A great deal of it has never been published before.

THE FOCAL ENCYCLOPEDIA covers completely the vast technology of photography and follows up all its uses for picture making. It defines terms, identifies personalities and quotes rules. It recalls past developments and records the present state of progress all over the world. It sums up scientific theory and instructs in up-to-date practice. It presents all the facts that matter, explains "why" and shows "how". It hands out advice based on first hand knowledge, expert skill and reliable authority.

THE FOCAL ENCYCLOPEDIA is specially written in plain, readable and commonsense English. It was carefully planned and set out in alphabetical order for easy reference. You will be able to find, instantly master and put to good use, all the information you need from whatever angle you look for it.

THE FOCAL ENCYCLOPEDIA is the only work of its kind in the world. A unique, up-to-date and universal source of photographic knowledge and an unfailing tool of practical help to any photographer, student of photography, professional and amateur, advanced and beginner alike.

THE FOCAL ENCYCLOPEDIA can take the place of a photographic library; and no library is complete without it.

See it at your bookseller's or photographic dealer's or write for full prospectus to Focal Press.

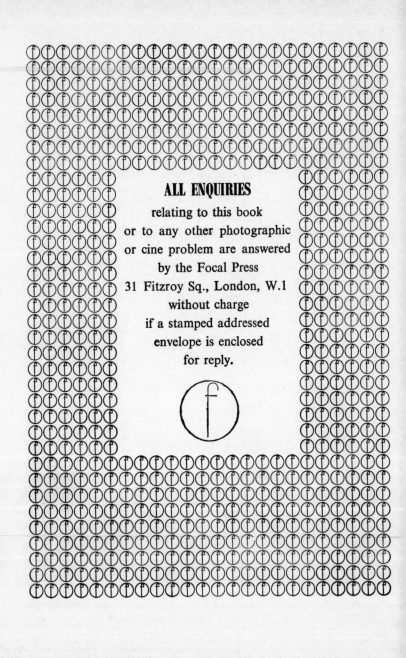

ALL ENQUIRIES

relating to this book
or to any other photographic
or cine problem are answered
by the Focal Press
31 Fitzroy Sq., London, W.1
without charge
if a stamped addressed
envelope is enclosed
for reply.